GALATIANS

GALATIANS: NAVIGATING LIFE IN VIEW OF THE CROSS

McKay Caston

STUDY GUIDE WITH LEADER'S NOTES

New
Growth
Press
newgrowthpress.com

New Growth Press, Greensboro, NC 27401
newgrowthpress.com
Copyright © 2023 by McKay Caston

Cover Design: Dan Stelzer
Interior Typesetting and eBook: Lisa Parnell
Exercises and Application Questions: Jack Klumpenhower

ISBN: 978-1-945270-19-2 (Print)
ISBN: 978-1-945270-20-8 (eBook)

Printed in India

31 30 29 28 27 26 25 24   2 3 4 5 6

CONTENTS

INTRODUCTION

Near the end of his epistle to the Galatians, the apostle Paul brings up one of the most natural human impulses: boasting. He says there are two kinds of boasting. One is boasting in yourself. You may do it aloud or secretly in your heart. You may do it smugly or you may specialize in its flipside of groveling and shame. The Galatians did it by assessing their outward devotion to Old Testament laws, but for you it may be other religious markers ranging from raw moral obedience to the quality of your prayer life. However you do it, your sense of worth comes from your performance and credentials. You boast in you.

The other kind of boasting is boasting in the cross of Jesus. You let go of your self-satisfaction with your achievements, and you rest in Jesus's achievements on your behalf. Paul knew he had to fix the Galatians' boasting so that they bragged about Jesus. Else there would be devastating effects. Individual believers would lose their joy. The fellowship would implode with infighting. And a spirit of mission would evaporate in the heat of self-righteousness.

Even if you're a believer, if you're honest you'll admit there are times you don't boast in the cross but find your worth in your performance. This means Paul's letter to the Galatians is for you. It's a gospel compass for navigating life with Jesus as your true north. As with the other resources in this series, you'll practice boasting in Christ from every point on the map, especially when waves of legalism threaten to steal your joy. You'll rediscover how God's saving, sustaining, and sanctifying grace guides the entire Christian life.

HOW TO USE THIS STUDY

This study guide is designed to help you learn from Galatians within a small group. Paul's letter was circulated among churches where groups of believers would hear it together and then work together to apply it. This means the insight and encouragement of your fellow children of God is part of the process. Pray for the Holy Spirit to work in your group. Make it a place where you are patient with those who need more time to understand and you sympathize with those who, like you, still struggle with weakness and sin. These attitudes fit the grace-filled message of Galatians.

Each participant should have one of these study guides in order to join in reading and be able to work through the exercises during that part of the study. The study leader should read through both the lesson and the leader's notes in the back of this book before each lesson begins. No other preparation or homework is required.

There are ten lessons in this study guide. Each will take about an hour to complete, perhaps a bit more if your group is large, and will include these elements:

BIG IDEA. This is a summary of the main point of the lesson.

BIBLE CONVERSATION. You will read a passage from Galatians and discuss it. As the heading suggests, the Bible conversation questions are intended to spark a conversation rather than generate correct answers. The leader's notes at the back of this book provide some insights, but don't just turn there for the "right answer." At times you may want to see what the notes say, but always try to answer for yourself first by thinking about the Bible passage.

ARTICLE. This is the main teaching section of the lesson.

DISCUSSION. The discussion questions following the article will help you apply the teaching to your life.

EXERCISE. The exercise is a section you will complete on your own during group time. You can write in the book if that helps you. You will then share some of what you learned with the group. If the group is large, it may help if you split up to share the results of the exercise and to pray, so that everyone has a better opportunity to participate.

WRAP-UP AND PRAYER. Prayer is a critical part of the lesson because your spiritual growth will happen through God's work in you, not by your self-effort. You will be asking him to do that good work.

In the collection of gospel-training resources created by Serge, Galatians has played a prominent role. The initial Serge resource *Sonship*, first published thirty-five years before the book you are holding now, largely grew out of teaching based on Galatians. The Lord used *Sonship* in a pivotal way to revolutionize my life and ministry with a revitalized understanding of God's grace toward me and his love for me in Jesus. I pray you will experience something similar with *Galatians: Navigating Life in View of the Cross.*

Lesson

1

THE JESUS-PLUS EQUATION

BIG IDEA

Even if we know the truth about Jesus, we can slip into trusting our own religious credentials instead, so that we need to be called back to the gospel.

BIBLE CONVERSATION *20 MINUTES*

The book of Galatians is a letter from the apostle Paul to several churches in the region of Galatia, in the center of modern-day Turkey. Paul had preached the gospel of Jesus there on his first missionary journey. He saw many people believe in Christ, including Gentiles who had never before worshipped the true God.* But soon after Paul moved on, false teachers infiltrated the churches he had established. Those teachers wanted two things: to avoid Jewish persecution Paul had experienced there, and to put trust in their own religious credentials.** They told Gentile believers that in addition to faith in Christ they should become Jewish by observing parts of the Old Testament ceremonial law, especially circumcision.

---

* See Acts 13:13–14:23.
** See Galatians 6:12–13.

The wider church's leaders soon met in Jerusalem to refute this Jesus-plus teaching. Paul's letter to the Galatians may have been written around this time. In his letter, Paul condemns the idea of adding Jewish law-keeping to faith in Christ. Instead, he teaches that we are reconciled to God through faith. Our righteousness before God is not something we *achieve* with any works on our part but something we *receive* by grace alone through trusting in the works of Jesus alone. The result of faith is what theologians call imputed righteousness, where Jesus takes on himself our record of sin and credits to us his record of perfect obedience.

With that background in place, have someone read **Galatians 1:1–10** aloud. Then discuss the questions below:

All through the passage, Paul references his authority and calling. What are some ways he describes that calling, and why does it matter for the topic he's addressing?

What are the reasons behind Paul's praise in verse 5, and how do they compare to the reasons why you praise God?

How do you feel about the strong words Paul uses in verses 6–10? Do they seem appropriate and necessary? Why or why not?

＊＊＊＊

Now read the following article. Take turns reading aloud, switching readers at each paragraph break. When you finish, discuss the questions at the end of the article.

Lesson

1

ARTICLE

SPEAKING THE TRUTH IN LOVE

5 MINUTES

Paul's letter to the Galatians is an intervention. He establishes a foundation of grace in his introduction, and then launches into some of the most forceful, pointed, and hard words he ever wrote. You've heard the saying, *the truth hurts*, but the truth is also meant to help. Paul loves the Galatian churches enough not to mince words.

In verse 6, Paul charges the Galatian believers with deserting Jesus. The Greek word Paul uses has the sense of putting something down and exchanging it for something else, like trading in an old phone for a new one. The Galatians were trading their previous understanding of what Jesus had done for a new perspective. This is why Paul exclaims in no uncertain terms that they are "turning to a different gospel," and that a *different* gospel is *no* gospel. This letter is a theological intervention aimed at restoring their understanding of the gospel.

The gospel will be *sola gratia* (grace alone) through *sola fide* (faith alone) in *solo Christo* (Christ alone)—or it will be nothing. Paul is willing to engage in the conflict of intervention because he loves these Christians. He knows that what we believe about the core message of the Bible affects every dimension of how we live. It impacts us at the level of identity. It influences both our outward actions and our inward emotional condition. If grace changes everything, so does the absence of grace.

A fundamental question each of us must ask is this: Am I standing on the foundation of *Jesus's* merit before the law of God, or am I standing on the foundation of *my* merit? Jesus is bedrock; our own merit is quicksand. Those who had infiltrated the Galatian churches after Paul left were teaching that Jesus did a lot to achieve forgiveness and reconciliation between sinners and God, but he didn't do it all. In other words, Jesus built most of the bridge over the rocky ravine of hell. All we must do is build our small part to complete the project. We call this a *Jesus-plus* doctrine of salvation. Jesus did his part; we do the plus.

Paul condemns this perversion of the gospel in the bluntest terms possible, pronouncing a curse on anyone who corrupts the gospel of grace by mingling human works into the salvation equation. The Greek word for curse is *anathema*, a term equivalent to saying, "Go to hell." Paul isn't being insensitive or snarky. By using *anathema*, he is stating that *Jesus plus* is a demonic corruption of the gospel. *Jesus plus* repels sinners and deceives believers by minimizing the cross of Christ. Since this false gospel of legalism has its origins in hell, Paul demands it go back where it came from.

The *Jesus-plus* equation is still alive and well. The plus is anything we look to for securing, sustaining, or improving our standing with God other than the blood of Christ and his imputed righteousness. Even very good things can deceptively become pluses when we think our performance of them make us right before God. For example, Bible reading and prayer are wonderful means *of* grace that could start to feel like means *to* grace. We might imagine that being diligent about doing these things somehow earns us God's approval.

For some, the plus may be our correct theology, a certain translation of the Bible, or the worship style we prefer. In pastoral circles, something as simple as what we wear—whether robes, jeans, or something in between—can become an unconscious plus that makes us feel we are rightly earning God's grace. We add to the righteous record of Jesus the fact that we are right about this or that.

For Paul, the *plus* problem was a big deal, like finding lead in the public water supply. Its presence was deadly and had to be eliminated at all costs. And the cost for Paul was the possibility that his intervention could strain his relationship with the Galatian churches. He knows he might face rejection, but he presses on anyway: "Am I trying to please people? If I were still trying to please people, I would not be a servant of Christ" (v. 10 NIV).

The only way Paul dares to speak the truth in love is with confidence that his own identity is not defined by what the Galatians think of him, but by God. Paul doesn't need the plus of the Galatians' praise. He isn't living to gain approval; he already has God's full approval in Christ. Paul knows Jesus didn't just do a lot, he did it all. It means Paul is set free from people-pleasing. He can love the Galatians by speaking the truth they desperately need to hear.

Maybe Paul's words are a gospel intervention for you. Perhaps you are like the Galatians and have added a plus to your salvation equation. If so, what an opportunity you have right now to confess and believe that Jesus really has done it all! This is the only path that lets you and I explode with adoration to God, like Paul does in verse 5. Paul is overwhelmed with gratitude. Mindful of his rescue and of the strong love of the Father to reconcile us to himself, Paul becomes a man on his knees with hands lifted high to God, "to whom be the glory forever and ever."

What will motivate that kind of response in your life and mine? Not a command or a law or guilt or fear. Not any kind of plus. Only the grace, kindness, and mercy of a God who does not rescue those who try to help themselves, but rescues those who can't help themselves. If you have never looked to the cross of Jesus with the kind of faith that sets your heart free and compels a similar expression of worship, I invite you to look now and believe.

DISCUSSION *10 MINUTES*

What experience have you had with necessary confrontations to defend the truth of the gospel? Did those go well? Why or why not?

When have you been truly grateful to Jesus instead of working to impress him with your credential? How has that affected your worship?

1

WHAT'S YOUR JESUS-PLUS?

20 MINUTES

Most believers regularly get tempted to add some kind of plus to their faith in Jesus. Whether that plus makes you feel saved, or is a way you convince yourself you're one of the *really* spiritual believers, it is confidence in yourself rather than in Christ. For this reason, it's healthy for you to recognize your own Jesus-plus tendencies so you can resist them daily and turn back to Christ alone. In this exercise, you'll work on your own to do that.

You likely have worldly credentials that make you feel acceptable to others—work, education, family, appearance, lifestyle, social codes, and more. But for now, focus just on *religious* credentials that make you feel right with God. Many of these will be good things meant to help you follow Christ, and they may be signs of your Christian growth. But they can also become Jesus-plus sources of self-trust if by them you sense you have earned your spot as an approved member of God's family. Even if you know better, that reflex to trust in the Jesus-plus remains.

Begin by reading each Jesus-plus item below. On your own, rank the items by how true they are of you. Assign the number 1 to the item that's most true of you, a 2 to the second-truest item, and so on. You will be asked to share some of your responses with the group at the end of the exercise.

___**Jesus plus my track record.** I might sense my right standing with God is based on my progress in holy living, my ability to act like a good Christian, or my level of success in battling certain sins.

___**Jesus plus my right alliances.** I might sense I get my right standing with God by my correct doctrine, my religious heritage, my church (or political) circles, my choice of worship practices, or the spiritual teachers I follow.

___**Jesus plus my feelings.** I might sense I get my right standing with God by the level of closeness I feel to him or some emotional fervor or sentimentality I reach during worship, prayer, or other spiritual activities.

___**Jesus plus my ministry.** I might sense I get my right standing with God from my Christian service, my involvement in the church, my success in ministry or mission, or my level of commitment to Christian causes.

___**Jesus plus my outward steps.** I might sense I've gained my right standing with God by some external act of devotion, participation in a religious event, or ritual sign of my decision to follow Christ.

___**Other:** _____

_____

Those self-based sources of confidence can never make you sure you are right with God, because only Jesus is good enough. Your righteous record is based solely on him. You cannot earn it by anything you do, but you receive it by faith alone—an inner confidence in Christ. In verses 3–5 of our passage, Paul describes how Jesus delivers you if your faith is in him. So now, finish by reading the gospel truths below that come from those verses. Select some that might especially help you abandon your particular Jesus-pluses and trust Christ alone.

- ☐ **"Grace to you and peace from God our Father and the Lord Jesus Christ."** Paul says grace and peace come to you from God. The Lord makes peace between you and him freely, out of his gracious kindness, releasing you from the burden to earn it.

- ☐ **"Who gave himself for our sins."** Paul says you are the recipient of a priceless gift. Only Jesus's perfect life could ever be enough to earn approval from God, and only his sacrifice could ever be enough to pay for every bit of your sin—and these are yours!

- ☐ **"To deliver us from the present evil age."** Jesus is your rescuer, in charge of finishing your salvation. As you fight your sin, you don't perform *for* him; you join his work *alongside* him. In his time, he will make you completely holy and remove all evil from the world, and you will enjoy the heavenly life with him.

- ☐ **"According to the will of our God and Father."** The entirety of your salvation, including your whole life going forward, is due to God's can't-change resolution to love you despite your own shabby credentials. You do not have a grumpy taskmaster eager to frown at you, but a loving Father who trains and protects you.

- ☐ **"To whom be glory forever and ever."** Your destiny is nothing less than God's glory. He gives what you could never earn: an unending life *with* him and *like* him. You will forever celebrate your rescue, not your own record.

When the group is ready, share and discuss some of your responses? What are your Jesus-plus tendencies? What parts of the gospel of Jesus especially help you to trust him alone?

WRAP-UP AND PRAYER *10 MINUTES*

Prayer is an essential part of a gospel-centered life, and a practice of faith. It is a habit of discarding all your own credentials and approaching your Father based only on how you are his child in Christ, and in Jesus's name receiving from God what only he can give. So now, exercise your faith by praying together to your Father. Ask him to use your time studying Galatians to strengthen your trust in Jesus and make you more like your Deliverer.

2

FACT-CHECKING THE GOSPEL

BIG IDEA

The doctrine that salvation is ours by faith alone in Jesus alone, with nothing we must do to earn it, is a message we can know is absolutely true.

BIBLE CONVERSATION *20 MINUTES*

In his letter to the Galatians, Paul has asserted that the only true gospel is one that adds nothing to the finished work of Jesus. This might lead his readers to wonder why Paul gets to say what doctrine is true and how he can be so sure of it. Paul anticipates this question, and launches into one of Scripture's most detailed accounts of how a biblical author learned what to teach and checked it for accuracy. He will make two main points:

1. Paul's teaching came directly from God. Paul will emphasize how he was not influenced by mere human teachers, even very good ones. The book of Acts tells us God spoke audibly to Paul when he was first commissioned and on some occasions later.* God may also have spoken that way during the period

---

* See Acts 9:4–6; 22:17–21; 23:11; 26:14–18; 27:23–25.

of learning Paul will mention here in Galatians, though surely Paul also learned from God by studying the Old Testament.

2. This does not mean Paul blindly trusted his own understanding of what God taught him. Paul will tell how in the end he checked with the top leaders in the church to make sure his message matched what Jesus had also told them. He will especially mention Cephas, the Aramaic name for the apostle Peter, and James the brother of Jesus. Peter was the lead apostle and James was pastoring the Jerusalem church.

Now have someone read **Galatians 1:11–2:10** aloud, or have a few readers take turns. Then discuss the questions below:

In verse 11, Paul says the gospel he preaches is "not man's gospel." What makes the good news of Jesus different from the kind of salvation plan you might have invented for yourself?

Which do you find most impressive about Paul: his willingness to be taught by God's Word, or his willingness to let other believers check his understanding? Explain why.

What was important for Paul and Peter to agree on despite their differing missionary assignments? Why are these matters of agreement important?

* * * *

Next, read the article. Take turns by paragraph reading aloud, and then discuss the questions that follow.

Lesson

ARTICLE

GUIDED BY GOSPEL FACTS

5 MINUTES

In our passage, the apostle Paul submits himself to a gospel fact check. After he had left the Galatian churches, the new believers had been duped by theological misinformation. Paul taught that to save sinners, Jesus did it *all*. But others were teaching that, while Jesus did *a lot*, there was still a part for Christians to play in their justified status before God. For the apostle, this false teaching wasn't good news.

Today, if you take a religion course at a secular college, the professor likely will make a distinction between the Jesus of history and the Christ of faith. The idea is that the life of Jesus became a legend that evolved into a myth. According to this narrative, Jesus was an ordinary man who died a horrific death as a misunderstood peasant with a messiah complex. It's further suggested that his followers later created stories of miracles to validate their claims of Jesus as the Christ, the Deliverer prophesied throughout the Old Testament.

Paul wants to show that such speculation is completely false. His gospel teaching was neither dreamed up in his own mind nor a product of hopeful groupthink among him and other followers of Jesus. Paul describes the historical circumstances of how the message he preached came to him directly from God, without any human input from potentially misguided believers. Then he tells how, in the end, he fact-checked his understanding. Paul's concern is to present a reliable historical record that overrules speculation about humanly-concocted doctrines and myths. In doing so, he validates the Jesus-did-it-all gospel.

Paul describes a specific trip to Jerusalem where he met with the other apostles. He had briefly connected with Peter and James years earlier, but now he would present his message to a theological examining committee. Witnesses to these events were Barnabas and Titus, two of Paul's ministry partners.

It's notable that Titus, who was not a Jew, was not made to undergo the ceremonial rite of circumcision in order to be considered a fully-accepted member of the church. The other apostles didn't make him add anything to the finished work of the risen Christ. The fact that Titus was received based on his profession of faith alone, apart from ceremonial observances, was a real-life confirmation of the gospel of salvation by grace alone, which the Jerusalem leadership also affirmed doctrinally. Paul says in verse 6 that they added nothing to his understanding of what God had taught him. His message passed the apostolic fact-check process.

Today, our need to be guided by gospel facts is just as vital. So, let's consider three practical implications of applying the gospel fact-check process. First, if you move to a new community, fact-check churches before you join. Don't assume a church holds to a Jesus-did-it-all doctrine of justification. Do they actually teach it? Do they use love and grace to motivate spiritual change, or do they use guilt and fear? Is our spiritual adoption central to their teaching of Christian identity? What is their vision for missions?

Second, introduce your intellectual doubts to gospel facts. Most of us will face personal doubts at some point in our spiritual journey.

Is Christianity really true? Can I rely on the gospel of grace to be a compass for my life? Or have I been deceived by well-intentioned but blinded religious fanatics who lived two thousand years ago? The facts of the gospel stand in the wind of any intellectual challenge. Isn't it encouraging to know that the Bible anticipates your doubts and treats them seriously? In fact, this is one reason why Paul takes time to explain how he formed his teaching and why it is trustworthy.

Finally, allow God's facts to overrule your emotional fallacies. By emotional fallacies, I especially mean how you may be tempted to feel that your Father is disgusted and disappointed with you. Rather than treasuring you, you imagine he at best tolerates you. And so, rather than looking to Jesus, you may find yourself doing things you hope will offset your guilt and regain your favor with the Father. Some religious traditions call this penance, a painful duty you hope obligates God to grant forgiveness.

For the Galatians, this painful duty was circumcision. For you, it could be beating yourself up with words of condemnation, supposing that adequate feelings of self-loathing will compel God to show you mercy. But this is not how the gospel works. Our guilt was nailed to the cross in the body of Jesus. He has suffered the painful duty in your place. He paid it *all*.

The cross proclaims that God forgives and accepts you, not because of your obedience and sacrifice but because of Jesus's obedience and sacrifice in your place. God is not disgusted. Far from it! He wants you to believe that you are forgiven and loved. You may not feel forgiven, but in Christ you are. You might not feel loved, but in Christ you are. You might not feel treasured by the Father, but in Christ you are. Sometimes, we need these gospel facts to override our emotional fallacies.

Our faith will often face doubts, both intellectual and emotional. You may be there now. If so, put yourself in the Galatians' shoes. Be the recipient of God's desire to convince you, right now, that the facts of the biblical record concerning the mission of Jesus are true—not legend, not fable, but historical realities. Confess your need for Jesus as Savior, and follow him as Lord. Be confident that he lived for you, died for you, rose for you, and now reigns. And give thanks that it is 100 percent grace.

DISCUSSION *10 MINUTES*

What secular explanations of how Christian doctrine was created have you heard? How have you reacted?

Are you more likely to have *intellectual* doubts that the gospel is true, or *emotional* doubts that God really could be that good to you personally? Explain.

Lesson

EXERCISE

2

THE BIBLE FOR DOUBTERS

20 MINUTES

Doubts are an opportunity to turn to God and let him reassure you of the gospel's truth. The Bible understands your doubts. God wants you to come to his Word again and again, be encouraged that he gives answers, and believe. For this exercise, you'll practice doing that by looking up one more passage of Scripture.

On your own, read through the two lists below. Pick either intellectual doubts or emotional doubts, and then pick just <u>one</u> Bible passage to explore from whichever list you chose. Read the passage carefully from the Bible. Think about how God is reassuring you that the gospel is correct, and be ready to share what you learned. The point is not for your doubts to disappear after reading one Bible passage, but for you to be encouraged that God understands your doubts and regularly addresses them.

INTELLECTUAL DOUBTS. The Bible anticipates you will need reasons to trust that its accounts and teachings are true. If you want to look more at how the Bible writers discuss these intellectual doubts, pick one of the following passages to read:

- **Jesus** himself faced questions from people who wondered if they should accept his teaching. To see one way he responded, **read John 7:14–18**.

- **Peter** directly addressed the idea that his accounts of how Jesus saves us were just made-up stories. To see his response, **read 2 Peter 1:16–21**.

- **The prophets** understood that people would question how their teaching was any better than the latest ideas that came from the surrounding world. To see one answer, **read Isaiah 45:18–21**.

EMOTIONAL DOUBTS. The Bible also anticipates you will need to be assured that God really is good, and that in Christ your sin is forgiven and you have a loving Father. If you want to look more at how the Bible addresses these emotional doubts, pick one of the following passages to read:

- **Fear** results when you sense Jesus is fed up with your sin and is out to condemn you because of it. To see what the Bible says about Jesus's approach to his people who sin, **read Hebrews 2:14–18 and 4:15–16**.

- **Pressure** results when you feel you need to bring proof of progress, or conjure up some level of sincerity, to show God you deserve his mercy. To see what the Bible says when you feel a need to make yourself worthy, **read 1 Corinthians 1:27–31**.

- **Insecurity** results when you feel God must be coerced into loving you. To see what the Bible says about God's heart for his children, **read Psalm 103:8–14**.

- **Despair** results when you feel your sin is too big or too entrenched to be forgiven, and you stop turning to God, perhaps feeling like a fraud. To see what the Bible says when you feel that despair, **read Psalm 32:3–7**.

Once you've picked a passage and have read it carefully, write a brief summary of how it addresses your doubts.

_____

_____

Now, briefly describe how the passage might be helpful to you as you face doubts.

_____

_____

When the group is ready, share and discuss some of your responses. What did the passage you chose say, and how might its message be helpful to you?

WRAP-UP AND PRAYER *10 MINUTES*

Rediscovering and continuing to believe the gospel is a lifelong process. As part of your prayer time together, ask your Father to teach you his truth. He loves to give good gifts to his children.

3

GOSPEL COACHING

BIG IDEA

The gospel of grace is not just right theology; it gives us the confidence in Christ we need to live rightly, and the correction we need when we live wrongly.

BIBLE CONVERSATION *20 MINUTES*

Paul has been defending the truth that we are saved through faith in Christ alone, not by any further credentials we might add. He has just finished saying he and the other apostles are unified on this matter, but now he will bring up a time this unity was tested. It happened when Peter (called Cephas) and other Jewish believers from Jerusalem visited Paul and his missionary partner Barnabas in Antioch. The Antioch church included Gentile believers and had launched Paul and Barnabas's missionary efforts to the Gentiles, though Paul and Barnabas themselves were ethnically Jews like Peter.

Paul will refer to "the circumcision party." These are believers who held onto their Jewish identity despite their new identity in Christ. Observant Jews would separate socially from Gentiles, neither entering their homes nor eating with them, but the Christian community otherwise often shared both homes and meals.* The circumcision party from Jerusalem retained their separatist Jewish lifestyle and also may have pressured Gentile believers to add Jewish requirements to their faith—dietary rules, circumcision, and festivals. Paul will insist this is wrong, since all believers are solely "justified by faith in Christ." *Justification* is God's legal declaration that a believer is forgiven of sin and credited with Christ's record of obedience, enjoying a right standing with God.

Now have someone read **Galatians 2:11–21** aloud, or have a few readers take turns. Then discuss the questions below:

What are some ways Peter was sinning, not just in his outward behavior but at the heart level? How well do you relate to those temptations?

What was Paul's response to Peter's sin? How does it compare to the way believers you know confront each other about sin?

---

* See Acts 2:46; 10:25–29; 16:15.

Paul describes himself as dead, and Christ as living in him. List several things about Paul that this passage suggests are "dead," no longer a controlling force in his life because Christ has supplanted them.

* * * *

Now take turns reading this lesson's article aloud, switching readers with each paragraph. Then complete the discussion that follows.

REGAINING GOSPEL BALANCE

5 MINUTES

I'm in awe of gymnasts. Olympic greats make an apparatus like the balance beam look easy as they jump and flip along a four-inch piece of wood. But they will tell you there's nothing easy about it. We are not naturally used to maneuvering on such a narrow surface. It takes years of practice and competitive experience to execute skills on a balance beam. And still, even the very best sometimes fall off. Like the apostle Peter.

Here in Galatians, Paul describes a period when Peter failed to act "in step with the truth of the gospel" (v. 14). Like a gymnast on the beam, he lost his balance. If it can happen to an apostle, it can happen to you and me. In fact, it happens easily because gospel living feels unnatural.

To act in line with the gospel is to live by grace. Serge founder Jack Miller boiled it down to points later made popular by pastor Tim Keller: (1) the gospel says I am more sinful and deserving of condemnation than I would ever dare to admit, (2) but through the redemptive work of Jesus on my behalf, I am more forgiven, accepted, and loved than I could ever dare to dream. While my sinful condition is far *worse* than I think, the gospel is far *better*. This frees me to come and die to myself, serving Christ's kingdom.[1]

But like we're not used to balancing on a four-inch beam, we aren't used to living by this grace. The default of our flesh is to live by merit, where we earn our own righteousness—through morality, success, peer approval, political victories, or a thousand other ways we feel we are right because of our achievements or alliances. For Peter, peer approval gave him that sense of righteousness. He stopped looking to Christ alone to make him right. He lost his gospel balance and fell off the beam.

To stay balanced, we must keep our eyes of faith on the cross. When we know we are recipients of gift-righteousness, we gain gospel confidence. Then we are enabled for a God-powered life of repentance, faith, humility, and love. But because living by grace is unnatural, it takes practice. Like gymnastics, it requires humility and teachability. Thankfully, it is not our own balance that sustains us in grace but Jesus's sacrifice for every fall we've ever made or will make.

This forgiveness gives us the freedom to confess our lack of balance, get back on the beam, and fix our eyes afresh on the cross. So much of what we do and say is influenced by our fear of what others will think of us. Peter faced a challenge: would the opinion of God define his identity, or would he live for the opinions of his peers? The fear of man had caused him to take his eyes off Jesus and sink.

To help restore his fellow apostle's gospel balance, Paul provides a master class in gospel coaching. Note that he doesn't appeal to a rule for Peter to obey or a psychological mantra to boost his self-esteem. Paul simply reminds Peter of a doctrine to believe. He reminds his friend, "A person is not justified by works of the law but through faith in Jesus Christ" (v. 16).

Peter's primary problem was *theological*. He had experienced a moment of gospel amnesia. He had forgotten that it was Jesus's blood alone that cleansed him of unrighteousness. It was not ceremonial observances or personal associations. In fact, the same blood made the Gentile believers clean in the same way—by grace alone through faith alone in the finished work of Jesus alone.

In Christ, Peter already had God's approval. He didn't need the approval of men who thought he was somehow better for also acting Jewish. He could shed his fear of their opinions, and start showing love to his Gentile friends by sitting at their table. Peter's experience shows us how gospel faith provides the kind of gospel freedom that results in gospel love. Or as Paul will say later, all that counts is "faith working through love" (5:6).

Through faith, we possess the same record of righteousness as Jesus. This justification is not something we earn or deserve. It is a gift declaration of God that serves as the foundational blessing for everything else in the Christian life. Paul describes this life of grace when he speaks of dying to the law and being crucified with Christ.

Dying to the law is a way to say, "I've given up trying to save myself." Being crucified with Christ is a way to say, "I believe my sins have been nailed to the cross." In combination, these two phrases act like a white flag of personal surrender to grace. To live by faith is to trust that God counts me as a forgiven, accepted, beloved son or daughter, not because of my works for God but because of Jesus's works for me.

This means faith is not primarily emotional. I believe what's really true about Jesus *despite* my feelings of guilt and shame. Faith is an objective lens. I look through that lens and see the truth that Jesus is my substitute in life and death. He is the Redeemer who bears the penalty for my sin and gives me a new identity. This connection of faith to truth is what sparks emotion. It satisfies the deep longing every human has for acceptance.

Consider a few simple takeaways that I hope will help you live in line with the truth of the gospel as you walk with Jesus: (1) Be ruthless about finding your core identity only in Jesus's imputed gift-righteousness. (2) Give no one other than God your Father the power to judge your righteousness. (3) Memorize Galatians 3:20 and repeat it to yourself often: "I have been crucified with Christ. It is no longer I who live, but Christ who lives in me. And the life I now live in the flesh I live by faith in the Son of God, who loved me and gave himself for me."

DISCUSSION *10 MINUTES*

When have you, like Peter, lost sight of the cross, pursued the approval of people instead, and had it affect your treatment of others? Describe what happened.

Who has a role in your life like Paul was to Peter, coaching you in the gospel when you lose sight of it? How coachable are you?

EXERCISE

CHRIST LIVING IN ME
20 MINUTES

Part of being crucified with Christ is dying to your old way of gaining favor. You used to *earn* approval by your own credentials or how well you could follow the rules (either God's rules, or rules imposed by yourself or others). But life in Christ means knowing you already have your Father's perfect love—not earned, but as a gift. This confidence in Christ frees you from trying to earn God's love, letting you actually obey him out of love. Your self-trust and self-interest die, and Christ lives in you.

On your own, read through the chart showing the difference between life in yourself and Christ living in you. Note some ways God has changed you so that you act like a Christ-living-in-me believer. Also pick some items that show how you would like to grow to reflect this truth better. Be ready to share some of your thoughts with the group.[2]

Life in Myself	Christ Living in Me
Approval seeking. I tailor my actions to try to win the praise of others.	Secure in God's approval of me, I am able to live for his glory, not my own.
Selfish agenda. I keep trying to earn God's love, so my motive to "love" others is actually self-serving.	My love for God and others is able to be genuine, anchored in my Father's love for me.
Self-power. I look to myself for the strength to love God and others, and I often sense the power is lacking.	I know that the power in me comes from none other than the Son of God, so I confidently step out in love.
Distance. God feels far from me, like a critic in the audience for whom I must perform.	God feels near to me, living in me so that my life is about working alongside him.
Demandingness. I create performance expectations, not only for myself but for others, so that I'm often critical.	My insecurities and need to feel superior are supplanted by my hope in Jesus, so that I lose the need to find fault.
Bitterness and self-hatred. I find it hard to forgive others or to enjoy God's forgiveness of me.	The core truth of my life is that my Savior gave himself for me; forgiveness runs through my veins.
Achievement focus. I judge my worth by the success of my efforts or the love others have for me.	I find my worth in the love God has for me, releasing me to love others regardless of worldly measures of success.
Independent spirit. My pattern is to work on godliness on my own, seldom turning to God or other believers for help.	My habit is to receive before I achieve, relying daily on God's grace through his Word, his church, and prayer.
Self-rule. God's commands feel like rules that constrain me, so I often decide I should ignore them and do whatever feels right and pleasurable to me.	My Father's commands are helpful and loving. They give me the best kind of freedom—not the freedom to do what I want, but the freedom to do what is good.
Coldness. I have little joy in Jesus, resulting in little interest to tell others about him or work for his kingdom.	The status and hope I have in Jesus give me joy despite setbacks, and excitement about his kingdom.
Anxiety. Fears and risk-avoidance tend to dominate my decisions in life.	Knowing I belong to Jesus in life and in death frees me to take some risks to serve him and love others.
Prayerlessness. Prayer often feels unnecessary, fake, condemning, or boring to me.	My life comes from God, and I am learning to pray to him in all my struggles and needs.
Cross-lessness. I have little daily appreciation for what Jesus has done for me (I "nullify the cross"), but a big awareness of what others think of me.	I find ways to be encouraged daily by the gospel, which God uses to help me live for him rather than for worldly goals.

When the group is ready, share some of your thoughts. Where can you already see that it is no longer you who lives but Christ who lives in you? Where do you hope to grow to better reflect how you are a Christ-living-in-me person?

What is a concrete, daily-life way you might practice one of your Christ-living-in-me items (for example, a way you might practice taking some risk to love others in your daily life)?

WRAP-UP AND PRAYER *10 MINUTES*

Prayer is a way to practice living by faith in the Son of God instead of by your own strength. Pray together that you would see where you lose gospel balance, would embrace the gospel when that happens, and would be willing to repent.

Lesson

4

THE ANCIENT BLESSING

BIG IDEA

The blessing of righteousness that comes by faith is an ancient blessing, God's good-news plan for all his people, now revealed everywhere in the world.

BIBLE CONVERSATION *20 MINUTES*

The Galatians had heard Paul preach the gospel and had believed, but then succumbed to false teaching that claimed they also must follow Jewish law to earn God's acceptance. Paul has just reminded them how Jesus was crucified for their sin, and how this means that any idea they might be saved by their own obedience to God's commands died too. Now he will point to Abraham to show that a right standing with God has always been by faith, never earned by our obedience. Abraham appears early in the Bible as the father of God's covenant people. Paul assumes his readers are familiar with some facts about Abraham:

- God gave Abraham several promises of blessing. The crowning promise extended well beyond Abraham and his physical descendants, the Jews, announcing God's intention to use Abraham to bring salvation to the whole world: "In your offspring shall all the nations of the earth be blessed" (Genesis 22:18).

- God's initial covenant-making ceremony with Abraham did not require Abraham to promise obedience in return. Rather, that event began with Abraham having faith in God's promises: "He believed the LORD, and he counted it to him as righteousness" (Genesis 15:6).

Paul will also quote several other Old Testament passages from Leviticus, Deuteronomy, and Habbakuk. These show that the demands of God's law—though fitting for a people created in his image—always left his people under a curse for their failure, and that faith was the real path to righteousness all along. Our right standing with God is given *to* us because it was earned *for* us by our Savior Jesus, who died a cursed death in our place.

Have someone read **Galatians 3:1–14** aloud, or have a few readers take turns. Then discuss the questions below:

How did the Galatians' basic approach to God change after they had been believers for a while? How common is that same shift today?

Verse 8 says Abraham heard the gospel, meaning "good news." As Paul explains Old Testament events and teachings, which parts sound to you like good news, and why?

What are some ways Paul answers the question *Why did Jesus die?* that are different from how you often answer it?

* * * *

Now take turns reading the article, switching readers by paragraph as you read aloud. Then discuss the questions at the end of the article.

AN INTERPRETIVE KEY

5 MINUTES

Of all the words that might be used to summarize the message of the Bible, one of them has to be *substitution*. If you've ever felt the Bible is too antiquated or complicated to understand, substitution could be the interpretive key that unlocks the entire Bible for you. It can let you make sense of the Bible, which then helps you make sense of your life.

In Galatians, Paul reminds us that reconciliation between God and sinners is never earned by anything we do for God. It is all about what Jesus has done for us. The heart of the gospel, and a central theme that runs through the Bible from Genesis to Revelation, is *reconciliation through substitution*. Reconciliation with God through the grace of substitution influences everything in the Christian life.

This is the theological assumption at the start of chapter 3, where Paul reminds the Galatians that they had virtually seen the crucifixion of Jesus with their own eyes. Although they had not been present for it in Jerusalem, Paul had clearly explained the cross in his preaching to them. He had been so clear in his ultra-high-definition presentation of Christ crucified that he responds to their failure to live out its implications with perplexed frustration: "Who has bewitched you?"

It was as if they were under a spell, blinded by demonic deception. To shake them out of the trance, Paul asks them to remember how they had been reconciled to God. Was it because of their obedience to the law? Let's say it together: "No!" It was through faith in the *substitution* of Jesus for them—as it is for us.

The Galatian believers had started their lives as Christians with eyes on the cross. But they had been deceived by the schemes of the devil through the false teachers who had infiltrated their churches. Because those teachers minimized the significance of the cross, the focus of these Christians' lives shifted from Jesus's work for them to their work for God.

To reorient them back to Christ, Paul recalls Abraham's spiritual experience. Since the false teachers in Galatia likely were converted Jews who demanded Gentiles become Jews in order to be reconciled to God, Abraham was the perfect proof that we are not saved by anything we do but through faith alone in what God does. If Abraham, as the father of the Jews, was justified through faith in the promise of God and not by ceremonial rites or by his own obedience, the same is true for all who are disciples of Jesus.

If anyone understood the centrality of substitution, it was Abraham. After believing the Lord's promise that he would be the father of a great nation through which the nations would be blessed, he and his wife Sarah were still without an heir until far beyond her childbearing years. Eventually, with what was a humanly-impossible conception, Sarah became pregnant with the child God had promised. They named him Isaac. He was their only son.

We can imagine the turmoil in Abraham's soul when God commanded him in Genesis 22 to sacrifice Isaac as a burnt offering, which is a sacrifice of atonement for sin. But with Isaac on the altar and Abraham's knife raised, the Lord called out to stop the sacrifice. Instead of Isaac, the Lord provided a ram caught in a thicket.

"Abraham went and took the ram and offered it up as a burnt offering instead of his son" (v. 13).

Did you notice the key phrase? The ram was sacrificed "instead of" Isaac. It's hard to miss the foreshadowing of another only son who would not be spared but would give his life as a upon a cross as the true and final substitutionary, atoning sacrifice.

The theme of substitution continues through the formalized system of sacrifice that was established when the people of Israel were formed as a nation. Rather than sinners serving the death sentence they deserved, animals were provided as substitutes to die in their place. But did the blood of sheep, pigeons, goats, and bulls really forgive their sins? No.

All the substitutionary deaths in the Old Testament taught the people of their need to trust in an ultimate sacrifice who would fulfill the promise of God to cleanse from sin and reconcile sinners to himself. That substitute would be the Messiah, Jesus. Just as lambs were slain and blood spread over the doorframes of homes in the deliverance of Israel from the oppression of Egypt, the Lamb of God would be slain to deliver all believers from the oppression of sin and the penalty it requires before a holy God.

Paul ties the Old Testament's demand for substitution to Christ's fulfillment of the demand. Neither the ceremonial law nor the moral law was a means by which we could attain a position of good standing before God. The law shows us our need for a substitute who could obey the law in our place and who would suffer the penalty the law requires. *This substitute is Jesus.* He was cursed on the rough-hewn beams of a Roman cross so we could be blessed as the forgiven, accepted, and beloved children of God the Father—reconciled through substitution.

Substitution unlocks every part of the Bible. The law reveals my need for a substitute and the gospel confirms God's provision of the substitute. To believe the gospel is to claim that substitute. It is to profess that, while I have failed the exam miserably, Jesus has achieved a perfect score. Through the cross, he has taken my record upon himself and given his record to me. Jesus's righteousness is *my* righteousness. I no longer have anything to earn. I have nothing to prove and nothing to fear. I am free.

DISCUSSION *10 MINUTES*

What emotional reactions do you have to the Bible's news that salvation from sin is based on a punishment-taking substitute?

When have you found yourself "under a spell" like the Galatians, forgetting a truth that had been precious to you when you first believed?

Lesson

EXERCISE

A PASSION FOR MISSION

20 MINUTES

This lesson's passage reveals why Paul is so passionate about his missionary calling and about getting the gospel right. In verse 14, he explains his purpose: "so that in Christ Jesus the blessing of Abraham might come to the Gentiles, so that we might receive the promised Spirit through faith." The word translated "Gentiles" also means "nations" or "peoples." Cross-cultural missions are not just activities some believers add to their faith. Rather, mission is God's big plan to save his people in every nation, announced all through the Bible and gloriously turned loose since Jesus ascended to heaven. Paul is excited to be part of *that*.

When you come to Jesus, you get caught up in his worldwide mission too. For this exercise, you'll work on your own to explore what's exciting about that mission and how your own passion for it might increase. Read through each item below. Then pick <u>one</u> item that interests you, and also look up and read the Bible passage that tells more about it. Finish by answering a few questions about what you read. Be prepared to share some of your responses with the group.

THE BLESSING OF ABRAHAM. Paul says Christ has brought the blessing of righteousness, which God gave to Abraham, to the nations. All people everywhere who hear the gospel and respond in faith are saved from sin's condemnation and freed from the burden of trying to make themselves right. What joyful news to announce! To see how this matchless message has been loosed for us to tell far and wide, **read what Jesus said after his resurrection in Luke 24:44–48.**

THE PROMISED SPIRIT. Paul says faith in Jesus also brings the very presence of God to be with those who believe. Banishment from life with God is the ultimate effect of sin, but God has come both to empower and to dwell with those who believe the gospel. To see how the coming of the long-promised Holy Spirit is a worldwide sensation, **read about the Spirit's arrival with new power in Acts 2:7–21.**

THE KINGDOM OF GOD. Paul reminds the Galatians how God "works miracles among you" (v. 5). Those miracles were a sign that the curses on creation, and the kingdoms of this world long kept in darkness, are now giving way to the kingdom of God where Jesus reigns in justice. To join in missions is to join the forward march of that kingdom, which will reach its full glory when Jesus returns. To see how the world's beastly kingdoms blaspheme God but are losing to Jesus, **read the prophesy in Daniel 7:23–27.**

THE WORSHIP OF GOD EVERYWHERE. Remember how Paul's endpoint is that saved people worship God, "to whom be the glory forever and ever" (1:5). To participate in missions is to join in the worldwide expansion of worship and the spread of God's famous glory—and there is no greater purpose than God's glory. To see how beautiful the global worship of God is, **read the prophesy in Zephaniah 3:9–13.**

What do you notice from Paul, or in the passage you chose, that shows how mission involvement is gratifying or exciting?

_____

_____

When we are uninterested in mission, it usually means the joy of God's grace to us and to the world hasn't penetrated us very deeply. Because God's grace feels small, we hold back from the sacrifice and risk mission entails. How might your view of the glory of mission work and God's goodness to you change if your heart were more personally and deeply affected by the kindness of God in Jesus?

_____

_____

Mission involvement is not just about going, but also about sending, training, supporting, funding, encouraging, praying, and more. What specific role or activity might God be calling you to do?

_____

_____

When the group is ready, share some of your responses. What did your reading show you, and what excitement for mission is God giving you?

WRAP-UP AND PRAYER _10 MINUTES_

As part of your prayer time together, ask God to give you excitement for being part of his mission and opportunities to get involved.

5

GOD'S MIRROR

BIG IDEA

God's law shows us our sin in order to draw us near to Jesus, not keep us distant.

BIBLE CONVERSATION *20 MINUTES*

Paul has been discussing God's saving promises, explaining that they come to all who receive them by faith alone like Abraham did. Now Paul will anticipate the objection, "But didn't God also give his people laws to obey that brought blessings?" Paul's answer assumes we know about some of the Bible's covenants, which are agreements between God and his people.

- **The covenant with Abraham** was put in place early in the Bible. God made **promises** directly to Abraham, the ancestor of the Jewish people and of Jesus. These include the promise of offspring (literally, "seed") and a home with God as an inheritance. God counted Abraham righteous because he believed. Abraham didn't need to make and keep any promises in return.* In that way, this covenant revealed how salvation

---

* See Genesis 15:1–21; Matthew 1:1–17; Hebrews 11:8–10.

has worked ever since the first sin: we are saved by God's grace, through faith.

- **The covenant under Moses** came several centuries later, as Abraham's descendants became an independent nation. God came down on Mount Sinai, with his holy angels present, and gave **laws** to Moses who then relayed them to the people who promised to obey.* Those laws included the Ten Commandments, detailed instructions for worship and for life in the promised land, and other commands found in several books of Scripture. Paul will say this covenant fits under the earlier covenant with Abraham, not canceling it or changing the fundamental way salvation works.

Have someone read **Galatians 3:15–25** aloud, or have a few readers take turns. Then discuss the questions below:

What makes God's promises marvelous and unrivaled according to Paul, so that you are astounded to be included in them?

What does Paul say about God's law that you can relate to in your desire to obey God?

---

* See Exodus 19:1—20:21; Deuteronomy 33:2–4; Acts 7:53.

How do the differences between living under a promise and living under law change the way you relate to God?

✳✳✳✳

God's law can feel like a confusing topic. So now, read this lesson's article, which will explain how to understand the law. Take turns by paragraph reading aloud, and then discuss the questions.

Lesson

ARTICLE

WHAT USE IS THE LAW?

5 MINUTES

A study of God's law in the Bible distinguishes between at least three kinds of law. Starting in the Old Testament, we are introduced to the *moral law*. This is more than merely keeping rules. Moral laws are objective, universal, and perpetual practical ways we love God with all our heart, soul, and mind and love other people with selflessness and sacrifice. Although summarized in the Ten Commandments, specific applications of the moral law are provided in more detail all through the Bible and find their perfect expression in the life and ministry of Jesus.

The second type of law we find in the Old Testament is *ceremonial law*. These laws provided clear directions for Jewish worship and festivals, especially the system of sacrifice. Plus, it listed clean and unclean foods and imposed cleansing rituals. When we arrive in the New Testament, the ceremonial law is fulfilled in Jesus, the Lamb of God and final sacrifice. We are made clean through his shed blood. Those laws that once pointed ahead with shadows of Jesus are no longer in force, since the Savior they anticipated has now come in the flesh.

The third category of law in the Old Testament is *civil law*. These laws functioned as case law that governed the citizens of Israel as a geopolitical nation pointing to the coming kingdom of Christ. With the New Testament, the civil law also has expired.[3] Now that God has proclaimed the gospel to all nations, his people and his kingdom are international. We can still learn from the civil law what sort of laws generally reflect God's justice, but the particulars were for a time that is now past.

With the ceremonial and civil law no longer binding for the church, our concern in this lesson is the moral law. There is a standard that defines what is true, good, and beautiful in contrast to what is a lie, evil, and abhorrent to God. The Lord is not only the Creator of the material universe; he is the designer of the moral universe in which every human lives. God's law is intended for our good. It sets boundaries for human flourishing. And it shows us how to reflect and glorify God, which is our created purpose and our end as redeemed people.

Yet, we often live our moral lives according to what is right in our own eyes. At the heart of human sin is a defiant resistance to submit and conform to the law of God. The question is, what will we do when we get caught? Will we make excuses? Will we try to defend ourselves. Or will we confess our guilt and obtain God's mercy?

Paul argues that Christians are not reconciled to God because we keep our promises to him, but because he keeps his promises to us. God's promise, announced so clearly to Abraham, is called the *covenant of grace*. It provides for our disobedience with someone else's obedience. We don't earn the promise. We don't deserve the promise. We only receive it by taking God at his word.

God could never retract that promise of grace, so Paul asks why the law was given later. The answer: "because of transgressions." Remember our tendency to be defiant. In Romans 3:20, Paul explains, "No one will be declared righteous in God's sight by the works of the law;

rather, through the law we become conscious of our sin" (NIV). The law functions like a police officer's flashing blue lights in our rear-view mirror. It tells us we have transgressed God's moral boundaries. There's nothing we can do but pay the fine—or have someone else pay it for us.

This use is the *redemptive purpose* of the moral law. Like a mirror, it helps us see how we have failed to love God and neighbor. The willful way we resist the law exposes a heart that hates the authority of God. Since God is our King, sin is nothing less than treason, and we know what the penalty is for treason.

But Paul proclaims good news for traitors: "Christ redeemed us from the curse of the law by becoming a curse for us." On a cross, King Jesus was counted a traitor in our place, suffering the penalty we deserve for our crimes against the very King who gave his life for the guilty. This is why Paul says in verse 21 that the law is not opposed to the gospel but functions hand in hand with the gospel. Faithful preachers will not preach law *or* gospel but law *and* gospel.

Paul calls the law our *guardian* until Christ came. That word can also be translated "schoolmaster" or "tutor." I like to think of the law as a professor of grace who knows that if repetition is the mother of learning, failure is the father. My failure to keep the law makes me run to Christ and embrace the wonder, beauty, and transforming power of God's grace in the cross. The law is not a cruel master, but a friend who wounds me to heal me.

So, the law is good. It reveals the will and wisdom of God, and it works with the gospel to show us our spiritual need. But the law cannot save. Trying to gain merit before God by being a good person is a fool's errand. Instead, the law leads us to Jesus. Like someone who wants to make an introduction between friends, the law says, "Sinner, meet the Savior." And Jesus says, "Sinner, come to me and find rest for your soul."

DISCUSSION *10 MINUTES*

Does God's law feel to you like a cruel master or more like a friend? Explain.

When you get caught in sin, are you more likely to think you must somehow "pay the fine" yourself or do you draw nearer to Jesus?

Lesson

EXERCISE

DRAWING NEAR IN PRAYER

20 MINUTES

As you grow as a Christian, God's law will show you what it looks like to be godly and, as you learn, also convict you. You will see your sin more clearly and deeply. Your response to this conviction of sin is important. Will you pull back from God in shame or fear? Or will you use conviction of sin as an opportunity to draw nearer to God in Christ, who took your shame and erases your need to fear?

A main way to draw near is to pray. Jesus gave a framework for prayer in the Lord's Prayer, found in Matthew 6:9–13 in the middle of his teaching about God's law. For this exercise, you will think about how you can use the items in the Lord's Prayer to draw near when your sin convicts you. On your own below, read each item and the conviction-based prayer that might arise from it. Think about the benefits of praying like that, and complete the two responses that follow. You'll share some of your results with the group when you finish.[4]

"Our Father in heaven, hallowed be your name."

PRAYER: Father, thank you that in Jesus you welcome me as your child even though I have sinned again. I praise you for your fatherly care for a wayward child like me. You are the hallowed Father who created every family in heaven and on earth. What a wonder it is that you have made me your eternally-loved child! I know you will love me wisely and well. Guide me, discipline me, reassure me of your kindness, and pour out the inheritance of grace on me.

"Your kingdom come, your will be done, on earth as it is in heaven."

PRAYER: Father, I confess that my desire for the beauty of your kingdom has been too small. I have chased after my own desires and glory instead of your greater glory. Grow my passion for a life that reflects you and brings praise to you wherever you take me in this world.

"Give us this day our daily bread."

PRAYER: Father, my sin reminds me again how needy for you I am every day. Give me all I need to live and, more importantly, to live *for you*. Make me hungry each day, not only for bread but for every word that comes from you. Nourish my soul well as I feed on your word.

"Forgive us our debts, as we also have forgiven our debtors."

PRAYER: Father, forgive my sin against you. I have committed treason in my heart, but save me from judgment and be my hiding place. Just as you have eternally forgiven me in Christ, now forgive me as my Father and restore my relationship with you. Give me joy in salvation, and cause me to treasure your forgiveness, so that I too become a forgiving person.

"Lead us not into temptation, but deliver us from evil."

PRAYER: Father, be my protector. Be the guardian of my heart, strengthening me by the Spirit's power in me so that I grow more and more to resist sin. And be the defender of my soul, shielding me from evil and all condemnation until the day you bring me into my eternal home with you.

RESPONSE #1: Look again through the prayers listed above, thinking about your prayer life. Which items are already a regular part of your prayers? Which items do you want to make more a part of your prayers? Be ready to explain why.

RESPONSE #2: Now pick one of the prayers above and expand on it. Compose your own prayer of a few sentences, based on an item in the Lord's Prayer, that fits your personal conviction of sin. For example: "Thank you for your gentle hand with me despite my harshness with my children," or, "Glorify yourself in my life by making me more truthful at work." In your sin, draw near to your Father.

My prayer is: _____

_____

_____

_____

_____

_____

_____

_____

_____

When the group is ready, share some of your responses. How might you turn to God in prayer when convicted of sin?

WRAP-UP AND PRAYER *10 MINUTES*

You might use some of your prayers from the exercise as you close in prayer together.

Lesson

6

WEARING CHRIST

BIG IDEA

In Christ, all believers have an equal and precious standing as dearly-loved, inheritance-owning children of God.

BIBLE CONVERSATION *20 MINUTES*

Throughout his letter to the Galatians, Paul has been refuting false teachers who claimed that believers who kept or adopted Jewish law-keeping earned God's approval that way. Paul has written that all believers who have faith like Abraham receive the promises of salvation in Christ, like Abraham did. Any notion that we are saved by some kind of law-keeping, or any other slavish burden, ought to dissolve now that Christ has come and a fuller era of gospel proclamation has begun.

Now Paul will show how this means neither Jewish lawkeepers nor any other group of believers should think themselves superior to other Christians. In most English translations, you will notice that Paul speaks of all believers, both male and female, as "sons of God." A son had legal rights as an heir in ancient Greek culture, so it's likely Paul chooses that term to emphasize the eternal inheritance all believers share in Christ. He does not mean to make women feel secondary by the use of noninclusive language. On the contrary, his point is to make sure they know they *are* fully included in every blessing Jesus secures for his people.

Have someone read **Galatians 3:25–4:7** aloud, or have a few readers take turns. Then discuss the questions below:

List several blessings this passage says all believers share as God's children. Which do you especially appreciate, and why?

In verse 28, Paul mentions divisions within Galatian culture that might cause some believers to think they are better than others. How do these compare to things in your culture that might make some believers feel superior?

Think about Paul's imagery in 4:7, where he says we are no longer slaves but sons. What is the difference between a slave's approach to God their Master and a son's approach to God their Father?

****

Now take turns by paragraph reading the article aloud. When you finish, discuss the questions that follow.

THE MACRO AND MICRO

5 MINUTES

The words *macro* and *micro* appear to be opposites but actually can be complementary. In literary analysis, for example, if you only study a small (micro) portion of a story apart from the larger (macro) storyline, you will not understand the author's purpose. Or if you only learn the overall theme but neglect to explore the details, you will miss the story's heart—how the theme plays out in the lives of the characters. The macro and the micro go together.

Uniting the macro and micro also applies to the Christian life. Most believers gravitate toward one or the other. They either focus on macro theological concepts, or they concentrate on the micro practical issues we face daily. But the theological and the practical were never meant to be separated. We need both doctrine and devotion.

Here in Galatians, Paul gives us both. He places our personal, individual stories within the context of the larger, redemptive story of God. Paul teaches us that this leads to a life of peace, hope, and even joy. We learn to rest in a restless world as beloved children of a sovereign Father.

The promise of God to Abraham is a macro storyline of the Bible. It is about God's mercy toward sinners through Christ. If we miss this, we will have a tragically incomplete understanding of the gospel message. We might slide back into the default setting of how humans think about and practice religion, what Paul calls "the elementary principles of the world."

These elementary principles are the common precepts of religions that enslave their adherents in the chains of works-righteousness. In this model, acceptance with God depends on moral performance and pietistic devotion. Even secular culture has a pantheon of gods to which we are as easily enslaved. We post online and obsess about the responses. We feel pressure to rise on the sales team, secure the lead role, or have a successful child. We want to be appreciated, recognized, and praised. If these things rule us, they eventually turn into our gods. And every god except Jesus will enslave you. Your life will be filled with burdens and fear, not the freedom and peace offered by Jesus.

In fact, this is the reason Jesus was born—to set us free from the legalistic works-righteousness of the world, whether the religious or the secular variety. Paul writes, "But when the fullness of time had come, God sent forth his Son, born of woman, born under the law, to redeem those who were under the law, so that we might receive adoption as sons" (4:4–5).

The phrase *when the fullness of time had come* is a macro truth of the gospel. It magnifies God's complete sovereignty over all history. Yet his sovereign grace extends to each person who has faith in Christ, as we become adopted children of God. It plays out in the micro world of our daily lives.

Human beings are not by nature children of God. All people are *creatures* of the eternal Father and *subjects* under his kingly reign. But sin makes us "by nature children of wrath" (Ephesians 2:3), spiritually dead and in need of supernatural regeneration. The children of God are those who put on Christ.

Imagine you have gone for a run before a dinner date. Your clothes stink with sweat. What do you do? You shower and change clothes. The process takes you from being unpresentable for a dinner date to presentable. The same thing happens when we put on Christ. Our garments were soaked with sin, unpresentable in the presence of a holy God. But Jesus took the stink of our sin upon himself, being clothed as it were with our unrighteousness. And he obeyed the law on our behalf to clothe with his righteous garments all who receive him.

To receive this, I confess the stink of my unrighteousness. I take off my rags with repentance, and I put on the merits of Christ through faith. I believe that my identity before God is no longer defined by the filth of my sin but by the beauty of Jesus. I am now presentable before heaven—forgiven, accepted, and treasured.

It's important to highlight the word *treasured*. After all, an adopted child is a wanted child. The Father didn't have to pay the excessive cost of the cross, but he did. He wanted *you* to be his.

The Enemy will do his best to convince you otherwise. He will accuse you, both through your conscience and through people who make much of your sin and limitations. But the cross says that when the Father looks on you as an adopted child, his forgiveness is complete and his love is unfailing. This is why there's no ranking system. Our identity is found in the merits of Jesus, not our ethnicity, social standing, gender, or any other distinction. We stand as one on level ground before the cross—perfectly forgiven, perfectly righteous, and perfectly loved. If you belong to Jesus, there is not a believer on the planet more treasured by the Father than you.

Finally, combine this with the macro truth of God's sovereignty. The Father who loves us so thoroughly is also in total control, leaving nothing to chance, unfolding his redemptive purpose through the rise and fall of nations and also through the day-in and day-out of our individual lives. We do not have to choose between a God who is loving or sovereign. He is both of these *together*—for me! That's the macro and micro. And when I embrace both, peace begins to flow like a river.

DISCUSSION *10 MINUTES*

Do you more easily believe that God is in charge of everything or that he perfectly loves you? Explain.

How often do you feel treasured and wanted by God? What besides the gospel tends to cause you to feel treasured, or to lose that feeling?

LIVING LIKE GOD'S CHILD

20 MINUTES

When you are secure in what it means to be a child of God, it changes your daily behavior. Instead of living for all kinds of approval and self-protection, the approval and protection you already have from your heavenly Father frees you to live for him and love others. You "wear" Christ—his righteous record, his heavenly inheritance, and his princely status as a son of the Ruler of the universe.

This exercise has two lists. The first is a list of child-of-God blessings found in this lesson's passage. The second is a list of daily-life situations. On your own, pick several situations from the second list that apply to you. For each situation you choose, match it with a child-of-God blessing from the first list that might be helpful for you to remember in that situation. Be ready to explain how your behavior in that daily-life situation might change when you remember how you are a child of God.

LIST OF CHILD-OF-GOD BLESSINGS

I am wanted. My Father desires me so much he redeemed me at the cost of Jesus's death on the cross.

I am wearing Christ. My right record and top credentials are already secure in God's eyes, due to my princely garments.

I am equally and supremely valued. Where it counts (with God) I am not superior to other believers nor inferior—nor can I be—since we all share the crowning honor of being his children.

I am an heir by promise. Without any pressure to keep deserving it, I have my Father's constant protection, loving guidance, and tender attention—plus a place in his eternal home.

I am no longer a slave to performance. I am free from the worldly principle of anxiously earning approval by my accomplishments or charm.

I am no longer a slave to non-performance. My sins, failures, and shame no longer define or control me.

I am part of a family. I serve God with an eager sense of ownership, as a family member who shares in my Father's grand mission.

I am Spirit-led in my heart. God himself is in me and beautifies my desires so that I long to be like my Father and with my Father.

LIST OF DAILY-LIFE SITUATIONS *(Respond to some that fit you.)*

When I am anxious about my performance at work/school/ministry/home, comparing myself to others rather than loving others, I can remember that as God's child I am . . .

_____
_____
_____.

When I am focused on being noticed instead of focused on others, or can't stand being overlooked, I can remember that as God's child I am . . .

_____
_____
_____.

When I get controlling or feel a need to have people see things my way, I can remember that as God's child I am . . .

_____
_____
_____.

When I feel condemned for my failures or sins, thinking I'm powerless to fight sin in my life or be useful to God/family/myself, I can remember that as God's child I am . . .

_____
_____
_____.

When I don't feel like obeying God and instead want to follow my own desires, I can remember that as God's child I am . . .

_____
_____
_____.

When I get tired of serving my family/church/workplace, and my self-effort approach to service wears me down, I can remember that as God's child I am . . .

_____
_____
_____.

When I seldom pray because I feel distant from God or have a self-reliant approach to life, I can remember that as God's child I am . . .

_____
_____
_____.

When I get corrected and bristle in response, so that others find it hard to teach me or love me well, I can remember that as God's child I am . . .

_____
_____
_____.

When I have little interest in missions or evangelism, or resist it because I fear what I may have to lose, I can remember that as God's child I am . . .

_____
_____
_____.

When the group is ready share some of your responses. What blessings might you remember, and in what situations? How might doing so change the way you act in that situation?

WRAP-UP AND PRAYER _10 MINUTES_

As you close in prayer together, remember that in praying you are putting your status as a child of God into practice. Tell your Father your needs. Ask him for his guidance. Thank him for his love.

Lesson

7

LIFE ON THE GOSPEL HIGHWAY

BIG IDEA

It's easy to get detoured away from gospel faith, which hurts our relationships and enslaves us to self-concern, so that we need constant reorienting toward Jesus.

BIBLE CONVERSATION *20 MINUTES*

Remember that Paul had founded the churches in Galatia, preaching the gospel of grace through faith in Christ alone. But false teachers arrived later, acting superior, and they convinced the new believers they were still outside of God's favor unless they kept Jewish ceremonial laws like circumcision, dietary restrictions, and the feast-day calendar. Paul has just finished saying this is a return to the earn-it approach to life, which enslaves us in failure. Now he will remind the Galatians of their former days with him, including mention of an ailment he had then. It's uncertain what this ailment was.

Paul will also write about the life of Abraham again, this time focusing on Abraham's sons. In Genesis, the Bible's first book of the Law, Abraham and his wife Sarah were childless and she was past childbearing age. Yet God had promised them a son through whom salvation blessings would come. In a lapse of faith, the couple decided Abraham should have that son by using Sarah's servant woman Hagar as a surrogate, and a son was born named Ishmael. Paul will use the son by Hagar as an example of trying to get God's blessings by our own doing, or "according to the flesh," like the false teachers' approach to the covenant laws given at Mount Sinai and the similar mindset in Jerusalem. Years after Ishmael's birth, God miraculously gave Abraham and Sarah a son Isaac through whom the covenant promises, including Christ, actually came. But Ishmael tried hold onto his firstborn status, tugging the family back toward a habit of laughing at God's promises by mocking the toddler Isaac, so that Hagar and Ishmael were sent away from the family camp.*

Have someone read **Galatians 4:8–31**, or have a few readers take turns. Then discuss the questions below:

If the Galatians' law-keeping practices are their way to show their devotion to God, why would those practices be bad? Explain Paul's reasoning.

---

* See Genesis 16:1–17:21; 21:1–14.

In verse 17, Paul says the false teachers "want to shut you out, that you may make much of them." How does this differ from Paul's attitude about ministry or from the Galatians' attitude when they first believed?

Based on Paul's sketch of Sarah and Hagar, why is it fitting that Jesus would come through the child of a woman who figured there was no hope she could manage to have a child?

****

Next, read the article aloud, switching readers at each paragraph. Discuss the questions that follow when you finish.

ARTICLE

REROUTING

5 MINUTES

I'm old enough to remember the days of the oversized road atlas. Rather than real-time navigation, you'd have a large book stashed under your car's passenger seat filled with pages of colored maps. Of course, you couldn't drive and flip through a map book at the same time. That would be like trying to scroll through a phone display or text while behind the wheel. And nobody would do that.

Anyway, one of the best features of real-time navigation is its ability to reroute you in case you take a wrong turn. In Galatians, Paul is functioning like that for a community of Christians who have lost their way. Having started their journey on the highway of grace, they have been lured into the dark alley of legalism. Legalism looks to our own merits as the foundation of our identity. It enslaves us under guilt and religious burdens. Paul knows the consequences of legalism are devastating to individuals, relationships, and churches. In view of such a dangerous detour, he reroutes us back to the cross.

Legalism is the default setting of the human heart. Paul calls it "the weak and worthless elementary principles of the world" (v. 9). These principles demand their adherents earn favor with God or with other people by meeting certain established standards. The "good" people who keep the law are in, and the "bad" people who break the law are out.

But with this approach, salvation loses its joy. During Paul's missionary trip through Galatia, he suffered a bodily ailment. The Galatian believers sacrificed a great deal in caring for him. Their practical concern was evidence of their love. They were glad for the opportunity to serve and bless Paul, the missionary who had sacrificed so much to tell them the message of God's grace in Jesus. But now Paul asks, "What then has become of your blessedness?" (v. 15). Their original joy was gone.

Can you see what a detour into legalism did? They were no longer capable of *expressing* love because they were no longer *receiving* it. Paul had preached that the love of God is a gift, but false teachers had turned it into a reward. This changes the motive for what we do. Why do I pray? Why do I give to the church? Why am I generous with others? Why do I share my faith? Why do I put my neighbor's interests before my own? Is it because I'm trying to earn approval—because I *should*? Or is it because I am compelled by the grace and love God has already shown to me? It's not that I *have to* pray—not in the sense of meeting some standard for God's favor—but that I *get to*!

This is why we sing in worship. It's not because we have to, but more because we can't help it! As our hearts are renewed by re-believing the gospel week after week, we stand on solid ground with gratitude and we overflow with praise.

Then why would someone who is free in this way want to go back to the drudgery of legalism? Because legalism is so subtle, so natural, we often do not realize it when we drift out of the gospel lane. The truth is that we need rerouting every day, and moment by moment throughout the day. The Enemy will tempt you into finding your value in your work, or your bank account, or your degrees, or your clothes, or your role in Christian leadership, or your involvement in the community. Satan wants you to find your identity in being right, so that you feel you must defend yourself or must win the argument, the game, or an election.

Even Abraham and Sarah succumbed to this for a time. They grew tired of waiting on the Lord to fulfill his promise, so they sought a more doable option—something they could perform to make God's blessings come to them. I have no idea how either Sarah or Abraham could be okay with a plan to have Sarah's attendant be the surrogate mother for their child. Actually, I don't think they were okay with it. I think they were desperate.

Have you ever been desperate? To fix something? To get people to like you? To get *someone* to like you. Desperate to relieve the feeling of sadness? Sometimes, desperate feelings prompt desperate measures. Rather than wait upon the Lord's timing, trusting his wisdom and his way to love others, we pursue our desires "according to the flesh." We choose legalism over grace, human works over faith.

In the case of Abraham and Sarah, God promised a son and then he—not they—finally provided Isaac. This is why Jesus was born as well: to do for us what we could not do for ourselves. People with an Ishmael-like spirit have a natural aversion to this grace. They try to hold on to favored status, mistreating "little brothers." They despise weakness. They are condescending to those they sense are inferior.

But grace reroutes us and says, "O sinner, you need a Savior! Run to Jesus. Look away from yourself and to the cross." When we heed this, we throw out every scrap of self-trust and self-glorifying spiritual pride we find in ourselves. We confess it and despise it, falling on our knees with praise and thanksgiving before our Savior, who took on the stink of our legalism to cover us with the aroma of his perfect righteousness. It is from such a posture that the Holy Spirit fills our souls with new motives and desires for obedience, and we live a new life with resurrection power.

DISCUSSION *10 MINUTES*

The article explains legalism as looking to your own merits as the foundation of your identity. What situations have caused you to drift back to legalism, even if you know the gospel?

How have you embraced personal weakness so that God's strength takes over in your life?

Lesson

EXERCISE

7

BEING A GOSPEL TRAVELER

20 MINUTES

The image of highway travel is a helpful way to think of your life as a gospel believer. At any time, you might take a **wrong turn** and place your hope in something other than Jesus. You find yourself in a **dark alley**, as your agenda to make your hope happen causes you to mistreat others like Ishmael mistreated Isaac. The solution is not to stop your behavior through willpower (since you can't), but **reorienting** yourself to believe the gospel again and trust Jesus anew. It's how you get **back on the highway** and are free to make progress in treating people the way Jesus treats you.

On your own, read through the examples of how this might happen. For each point in the "detour," pick an item that fits your personal spiritual path, and give a more specific description. Be ready to share some of your responses.

WRONG TURN. Where besides Jesus might you be looking for your sense of core identity, worth, and acceptance? It might be:

- Some religious or ministry achievement, superiority, or service
- A career, workplace, or community success/ability

- Some kind of family approval, prosperity, reputation, or contentment
- A close relationship, circle of friends, or admiring community
- Alignment with the right political, social, or religious camp
- Being "yourself" (You sense your identity depends on expressing what feels right to you rather than the freedom you have in Jesus to be like him.)
- Your competence, survival skills, or ability to provide
- Someone's love, appreciation, or notice
- Something else

My wrong turn is _____

_____.

DARK ALLEY. How has your desperation to grasp or to guard that sense of worth affected your relationships, so that self-protection drives your treatment of others? It might be:

- A compulsion to look good compared to others, or in front of others
- An urgency to be "first in line" or not miss out
- A need to always be right—making you not teachable, or risky to confront
- An urge to control the situation or other people's choices
- A tendency to criticize, boast, or complain
- Withdrawing from people or avoiding duties when you might fail or be exposed
- Exhaustion from people-pleasing, or discouragement when it doesn't work

- Little desire to pray for others or tell them about Jesus
- Little desire to pray for yourself or request prayer, which requires a posture of weakness
- Something else

My dark alley is _____

_____.

REORIENTING. Now remind yourself how perfectly Jesus gives you the sense of identity, worth, and acceptance you crave. What can you re-believe about Jesus and who you are in him that will teach your heart not to take your wrong turn? It might be:

- One of the blessings of being God's child that we've seen in Galatians
- An aspect of God's absolutely free gift of forgiveness and righteousness
- An encouragement stemming from how God is with you to help and comfort you, not distantly assessing you
- A part of the eternal inheritance you possess and will enjoy in the heavenly life
- Something else

To reorient, I will remember _____

_____.

BACK ON THE HIGHWAY. Now that you are back on the gospel highway, how might your relationships and treatment of people become more Christlike? You will *get to* pursue that change, but don't let your progress become your source of worth. Keep believing the gospel, rest in Christ, and work prayerfully as you draw on *his* power—he lives in you.

I get to change to be more _____

_____.

When the group is ready, share and explain some of your responses. What is your wrong turn away from the gospel? What is your dark alley? What is your rerouting? What change do you hope to see when you are back on the gospel highway?

WRAP-UP AND PRAYER *10 MINUTES*

Pray for each other and request prayer for yourself, that God would give you faith daily and make you more like your Savior.

8

THE KNOT OF GRACE

BIG IDEA

Spiritual disciplines are important ways we turn regularly to God and receive his help—his grace—but they must not become religious badges by which we spurn grace and try to earn our own righteousness.

BIBLE CONVERSATION *20 MINUTES*

The Galatians have been looking to their religious performance to feel good about their standing with God, and Paul has been condemning this. Now he will point out one religious rite in particular: their trust in being circumcized. Circumcision was part of the Old Testament ceremonial law that pointed to Christ and is no longer in effect. But Paul's chief concern is *any* trust in any kind of religious performance or duty that undermines faith in Christ himself. Many religious practices are good. But Paul will say that trying to earn a righteous record by these practices is misplaced faith in ourselves. It means we are choosing the impossible obligations and slavery of law-keeping, which cuts us off from Jesus's righteousness that comes by grace.

Have someone read **Galatians 5:1–12** aloud, or have a few readers take turns. Then discuss the questions below:

What kind of freedom does Paul mean when he says Christ has set us free, and how is it different from other ways you think about freedom?

If "neither circumcision nor uncircumcision counts for anything" (v. 6), why is Paul so opposed to those who advocate it and so insistent that the Galatians refuse it?

There are two kinds of offense at the end of the passage: those pressing for circumcision are troubling the Galatians, while Paul is preaching the offense of the cross. What's the core difference between those two kinds of offense?

****

Now take turns reading the article aloud, switching readers with each paragraph. Discuss the questions when you finish the article.

Lesson

ARTICLE

ONE VOICE TO RULE THEM ALL

5 MINUTES

In 2011, the *New York Times* featured a story about a fifty-one-year-old ex-convict named Robert Salzman.[5] Salzman had spent his entire adult life in prison, but following his release he eventually found work as an actor in a film, playing the role of a hardened former prisoner. It was a solid, paying job, and he finally felt free.

Late one afternoon, after a long day of filming on location in a Long Island penitentiary, Salzman fell asleep on a cot in a prison cell. He woke up disoriented. Seeing the bars, he began to weep uncontrollably, thinking his freedom had been a dream and he was a prisoner again. But he wasn't a prisoner. That cell wasn't his real home and that cot wasn't his real bed. He could walk out of that cell anytime he wanted. He was free—but for a moment he forgot it.

Every true, regenerate believer is like Robert Salzman. We too have been released from prison. Legally, before heaven, we are free of all charges because Jesus served the penalty we deserved for our treason against the King. But believing our sentence has been fully served and satisfied by Jesus is not easy. We can become disoriented, thinking the verdict of God has been overturned by accusations from Satan, or from someone who makes much of our faults, or from our own conscience.

Lamentations 3:23 reminds us that the Lord's mercies "are new every morning." This is the purpose of what many Christians call morning devotions. Reading Scripture and prayer are not burdensome duties we must fulfill. They are means for remembering the mercies of God in Jesus that are ours every morning of every day. Morning prayer and communing with God throughout the day are how we constantly realign our minds, hearts, and souls to the truth that Jesus's blood has set us free.

When not treated as a merit-earning obligation, prayer is such a good thing! It lets us speak freely with a sovereign Father whose love for us is higher, deeper, broader, and wider than we can comprehend. It is nourishment for the soul. Spiritual disciplines like prayer and feeding on God's Word—both reading Scripture and hearing it preached— are called *means of grace*. They are opportunities to experience more grace from God.

But this freedom can be a fight. We so easily take our eyes off the work of Jesus and become fixated with our own religious merits. Then our prayers become cold and worship is lifeless. We may feel a great deal of religious duty about these disciplines, but not joy and rest—much less a genuine love for God. This is what legalism does. It appeals to spiritual pride, and so it destroys the soul by unlatching our faith from Jesus. We become spiritually insecure, constantly comparing ourselves to others for a sense of standing before God. Am I doing as much as they are? Am I doing it as well as they are?

Paul says, "This persuasion is not from him who calls you" (v. 8). Anything that loosens the knot of grace, even if it's an otherwise-good religious thing, is not of God but of the devil. What matters to God is not what righteousness I can claim within myself, "but only faith working through love" (v. 6). We love because God first loved us. And being the recipient of unearned love empowers us to express the same kind of love to others.

We pray for people who persecute us. We feed them and clothe them. We tend to their material needs as the spiritual seeds of grace bloom in our hearts. And God receives all the credit for the love that flows through us, since it was his love that flowed to us in the first place. The issue is not whether we are more right or more diligent or more *whatever* than someone else, but whether our faith is moving outward to others in a way that blesses them even if it costs us.

This means that our primary "work" is to receive grace upon grace by faith, which the power of the Spirit within converts to the fruit of love. If there's no fruit of love, the problem usually can be traced back to faith. If not motivated by gospel faith, our prayer, Bible reading, churchgoing, and other practices of receiving grace from God may easily become clogged with a legalistic spirit, like with the Galatians.

All of these spiritual practices are designed for us to hear the pardoning and accepting voice of the Father over and over. But there are so many other voices that compete with the Father's pardoning voice. Early in my pastoral ministry, a couple in the congregation I was pastoring informed me they had decided to find another church. During the exit interview, I asked what had influenced their decision.

All their reasons had to do with my inadequacies as a pastor. They listed their complaints and compared me to other pastors whom they considered more effective. I waited until their car was driving away before I broke down weeping. With this verdict on my ministry, I felt like a complete failure, imprisoned under their judgment.

But in that moment, I heard my Father's voice. It was as if I had been transported to the courtroom of God to stand before the Judge to face those accusations, many of which were true. As it turns out, Jesus was there too, looking upon me like a proud big brother, waiting to hear the verdict declared again, just because I needed to hear it again. Then the Voice of voices—the One Voice to rule them all—*my Abba's voice* spoke with a gentle, purposeful clarity from behind the bench, pointing toward me with open hands, saying, "This is my son, whom I love and with whom I am well pleased!" And I was free.

DISCUSSION *10 MINUTES*

What other voices in your life have caused you to turn your eyes away from Jesus and to your failures?

What religious successes or practices have caused you to turn your eyes away from Jesus and to your merits?

Lesson

8

SPIRITUAL DISCIPLINES AND YOUR HEART

20 MINUTES

When you pray and listen to God's Word, you put your faith into practice. As you make these spiritual disciplines a regular part of life, you repeatedly turn aside from your own strength and wisdom and merits. You rely on God's strength and wisdom and on Jesus's merits. This makes these disciplines an important part of a gospel-centered life. Believers practice them privately, with family or small groups, and in whole-church worship services.

But your remaining sin and the lures of the world fight against your desire to pray and listen to God's Word. Also, the devil loves to corrupt the best things, so you will be tempted to give these healthy habits an unhealthy role in your heart. Prayer and listening to God's Word might become either (1) a way you pride yourself for your religious commitments or (2) a reason you feel condemned due to your poor routines. The solution is not to give up those good spiritual disciplines, but to tune your heart.

On your own, complete the assessment of how your heart approaches these spiritual disciplines. Consider both your private Bible reading and prayer life, and how you feel about doing these disciplines with others. At the end of the exercise, you'll share some of your responses.

Concerns. First, what makes these disciplines difficult or distorted? Note some that are especially true of your heart.

☐ My devotion or right methods make me feel superior to others.

☐ My neglect or amateurishness make me feel inferior to others.

☐ These disciplines feel like a duty for which I earn or lose points with God.

☐ These disciplines feed my theological or devotional pride. My real purpose is not to seek God, but to feel good about becoming an expert Christian.

☐ I'm not aware of the importance of these disciplines, or I've been told it's unhealthy to make too much of them.

☐ I resist because I'm cold to God or uninterested.

☐ I pull back because I've been hurt or disappointed by religion and I'm not sure God can overcome that hurt.

☐ I'm drawn away by laziness, entertainments, or self-indulgence.

☐ My feeling that God is disappointed has caused me to give up in shame or despair.

☐ My feeling that I'm free to do whatever I want has made me lax.

☐ These disciplines feel like self-help activities that would probably be good for me if only I had the time and commitment.

☐ These disciplines feel self-indulgent, distracting me from real work and ministry I have to get done.

☐ I do it because I can't expect much goodness from God if I don't show evidence of my sincerity.

☐ Since it's hard for me, I figure it must not be working for me.

Encouragements. Now, what do you see in your heart that encourages you about these disciplines, or what would you like God to work in your heart? Again, pick several.

☐ It's an honor, joy, and comfort to be invited to work on my personal relationship with the loving Lord of heaven and earth.

☐ Like with a marriage, I'm eager to spend time with my Lover and know the investment is worth it.

☐ I love God and love being around others who love God too.

☐ I discover such beauty in the Bible and in prayer!

☐ God gives me saneness and rest amid all the craziness in the world and in me.

☐ God "flips on the lights" in the darkness—I see him and myself clearly.

☐ I really feel the need to put my struggles, which are too big for me to handle, into God's hands daily.

☐ I truly desire to have God's Word and the Spirit level me—bring me down from pride and raise me from despair.

☐ These disciplines are a lifeline I need, and fuel for my engine.

☐ The demands of work, family, and ministry draw me to spend more time with God.

☐ I come to God as a wanted child of the Father who is tenderly near to give, guard, and guide.

☐ I come to God imperfectly, *in* my sin and coldness and shabby discipline, and I know that's okay—it's much of the purpose of coming to God in the first place.

☐ My weakness is not an obstacle to God but a normal condition, and with the Spirit's help I cry "Abba! Father."

☐ Prayer and Bible learning are themselves a beautiful way to be like Jesus, whose life was filled with these activities.

☐ It's hard for me but, like all the best relationships and growth, so worth pursuing.

When the group is ready, share some of your responses. Try to explain what they reveal about your heart: for example, no time for God might reveal self-dependence, or no enjoyment of God might reveal little awareness of his goodness and love. How do you desire to grow?

WRAP-UP AND PRAYER *10 MINUTES*

Spend time praying for your Bible reading, sermon listening, and prayer life. Ask your Father to refresh your approach to them, make them a joy, and use them to make you more like Jesus.

THE FLESH-KILLING SPIRIT

BIG IDEA

The sinful desires of our flesh are still at war with the godly desires of the Holy Spirit, as we who belong to Christ kill off the flesh and walk by the Spirit.

BIBLE CONVERSATION *20 MINUTES*

Paul has been pointing out the two different ways to approach God:

- The **faith** approach trusts in Christ. It is powered by the work of the Holy Spirit.
- The **flesh** (*sarx* in Greek) approach is the impulse to resist Christ and find life in ourselves. It can take a *religious form* when we hope to earn God's favor by our obedience, our religious observances, or—in the case of the Galatians—even what we've done to our bodies. Or it can take a *rebellious form* when we give rein to sinful desires.

You will notice that Paul calls both the religious form of the flesh and the rebellious form of the flesh the same thing: they are both simply *the flesh.* They both stem from our rejection of Jesus, and so these two impulses are connected. Paul has just finished pointing out that the false teachers who advocated trust in self were also troubling others in the churches. Their earn-it religion paired naturally with uncaring sin.

So now, Paul will focus on a further benefit of the flesh-busting life we have in Jesus by faith. We are not only credited with Jesus's righteous record, but are also transformed by the Spirit into people who actually begin to love God and neighbor like Jesus. Our freedom from having to save ourselves comes with a larger freedom from all sinful indulgence. Our lives bear fruit that even the most rigorous of God's laws will not condemn.

Have someone read **Galatians 5:13–26** aloud, or have a few readers take turns. Then discuss the questions below:

Look at the description of the two sides of church life in verses 13–15. How does it compare to church relationships you've known?

Notice the variety of works of the flesh in verses 19–21. In your experience, why do they go together?

What do you find especially appealing about the fruit of the Spirit (vv. 22–23) when compared to the works of the flesh? What makes the spiritual life inherently beautiful?

****

Read the article next, taking turns by paragraph to read it aloud. Then discuss the questions that follow.

ARTICLE

TARGETING THE WRONG ENEMY

5 MINUTES

On a Saturday night in July of 2013, a fight broke out in a Chicago neighborhood. Someone identified a passing car as belonging to a rival gang and threw a brick at it. In retaliation, the car sped up and swerved into the crowd, striking and killing twenty-year-old Jose Ibarra. Soon his friends realized they had made a terrible mistake. The car didn't belong to a rival, but to someone in their own group. Jose was the victim of friendly fire.

The same thing can happen in a local church, or within marriages, or among roommates. It's possible for us to turn on our own, injuring each other with a similar kind of friendly fire. Most of the time, just like the death in Chicago, friendly fire among Christians is a case of misidentifying the real enemy. The true antagonist is not my spouse. It is not someone at work. It is not that fellow believer or that stubborn neighbor.

Whom does that leave? Paul writes, "The desires of the flesh are against the Spirit, and the desires of the Spirit are against the flesh, for these are opposed to each other, to keep you from doing the things you want to do" (v. 17). The enemy is my own *sarx*.

Paul attributes the relational chaos in the Galatian churches to the outworking of the flesh. Some believers were deceived into putting personal freedom above serving each other with sacrificial love. The sinful nature creates constant opportunities to throw bricks at the wrong car, creating conflict that could be avoided if we took aim at the right culprit. Since each of us is a natural-born brick thrower, the sooner we recognize the true enemy is the flesh, the sooner healing and restoration can take place.

It seems these days as if the flesh is on a feeding frenzy. Whether on television or social media, people are biting and devouring each other with accusations and insults. It is tearing communities, churches, and families apart. But who is the real enemy? Who should be on my short list of suspects? My flesh.

What if I took this seriously? What if I believed my biggest problem is not with you but is in me? How would that change our relationship? How would it change how I parent my kids and how I engage with fellow believers and with the world as an ambassador for Jesus? I can think of a few ways.

First, an awareness of my flesh will cause me to suspect myself before I charge someone else. You know how crime shows work. Suspects are ruled out one by one until the true culprit is arrested. An awareness of my flesh should cause me to suspect first that *I* could be guilty. What percentage of marital strife would cease if I were to interrogate my flesh before I investigated my spouse? What flames of accusation and insult could be extinguished if I checked my own heart? What wars would cease in the church if we stopped blaming, and were honest about the prideful self-rightness that lurks within?

Second, an awareness of the flesh means I consciously submit to the influence of the Holy Spirit. Paul says to "walk by the Spirit" (v. 16), which suggests moving forward with a purpose. Whatever the path before me, I will be led either by my flesh or by the Spirit. Will

I confess *my* sin or *their* sin? Will I forgive as I have been forgiven, or will I deny the cross and become embittered? Will I give grace or withhold it? Will I respond to the comment with empathy and kindness or with venom and snark? Will I display the dead works of the flesh or produce the living fruit of the Spirit?

Third, an awareness of the flesh will drive me to continually crucify my flesh with ongoing repentance. Paul writes, "Those who belong to Christ Jesus have crucified the flesh with its passions and desires" (v. 24). While the crucifixion of the flesh takes place initially at conversion, the components of the process are ongoing because of what repentance is. The English word is translated from the Greek word *metanoia*, which literally means "a turning" or "a change of mind." In repentance, we see our sin for what it truly is.

Sin is not an easy-to-make mistake or the mere breaking of a rule. It is a treasonous act of willful defiance against the wisdom and ways of the King—the very King who loved us unto death by suffering the penalty our sins deserved. Ongoing repentance is a change of mind from moral hypocrisy to moral honesty. I no longer hide my sin in the dark through denial, minimizing, or making excuses. Instead, I bring it into the light with a deep sense of grief and hatred for it.

In repentance, I do not turn first *from* my sin to Jesus (as if repentance were a promise to do better next time), but I turn *with* my sin to Jesus. In that moment, as I believe my sin "is nailed to the cross and I bear it no more," the Spirit fills me with a new love for the wisdom and ways of Jesus and a new ability to walk in those ways. In this way, repentance and faith kill the weed of sin, not just above ground but at the root.

DISCUSSION *10 MINUTES*

What are some situations in your life where you could look at yourself first rather than injure others? How would this be helpful?

What is a specific way you might consciously submit to the influence of the Holy Spirit in your life's daily routine?

Lesson

EXERCISE

FRUIT-OF-THE-SPIRIT PRAYER

20 MINUTES

If you were already familiar with the fruit of the Spirit, you may have learned to treat it like a to-do list. But studying the fruit of the Spirit in the context of Galatians reveals something different. The fruit is actually a description of what grows by God's power in a person who has repented of a to-do-list approach to God.

This means your efforts to love, be joyful, live at peace, be patient, and so on are done in a way that's always coupled with faith. You receive *from* God instead of performing *for* God. So, for this exercise you will pray. On your own, use the fruit of the Spirit as a framework for some personal time with your Father. Let the directions below guide you as you silently pray through the fruit three times: first **thanking** God, then **confessing** your sin, and finally **asking** for spiritual growth. Take about three minutes for each step. At the end, you'll discuss your prayer experience.

THE FRUIT FRAMEWORK *(For Reference)*

Love — selfless, sacrificing devotion to others

Joy — deep delight in being aligned with God

Peace — both peace with God and a peacemaking life

Patience — contentedly setting aside your own agenda and timetable

Kindness — warmth, care, and compassion for others

Goodness — contributing good to the world by doing good to others

Faithfulness — loyalty to people and promises

Gentleness — tenderness that lets others rest and be comforted

Self-control — discipline to walk by the Spirit, not gratify the flesh

STEP 1: GIVE THANKS. The Spirit's role is to make you more Christlike, so the fruit is first of all a description of Jesus. Go through the description. At each point, praise God that Jesus is like that toward you and has lived that way for you. (Take about 3 minutes.)

STEP 2: CONFESS. Admit your sin and how you fall short of each part of the fruit description. Express your sorrow to your Father, who is kind to the brokenhearted. (Take about 3 minutes.)

STEP 3: RECEIVE. Ask God to work in your heart by the Spirit, so that this kind of life grows in you. You might mention specific situations where you want each part of the description to flourish. (Take about 3 minutes.)

When the group is ready, tell about the prayer time you just had. What was encouraging about it, and why?

WRAP-UP AND PRAYER *10 MINUTES*

Group prayer is a natural companion to private prayer, so expand your prayer from the exercise to include spoken-aloud prayer you do together.

Lesson

10

DOING GOOD AND BEARING SCARS

BIG IDEA

Spirit-led people have a hope in Christ and a focus on his kingdom that results in a new approach to life's daily issues and to their dealings with others.

BIBLE CONVERSATION *20 MINUTES*

Paul has repeatedly said how false teaching that pressured the Galatians to trust in their religious observances (what we do for God) is far different from the true gospel, which is that we are saved by faith in Jesus alone (what God does for us). Now Paul will end his letter by showing more ways this difference plays out in how we treat each other, and by repeating the importance of trusting Jesus only. He has labeled self-trust and the self-concerned life that accompanies it living by the *flesh*. Trust in Christ is God-centered and God-powered, and Paul calls it living by the *Spirit*.

There is a sense in which the false teachers were trusting in their literal flesh, since one of the rites they pressed upon believers was circumcision. Paul will say that his body bears marks too—the marks of Jesus. This may be a reference to injuries from persecution, which the false teachers tried to avoid by making the churches in Galatia follow Jewish practices. The book of Acts tells us that when Paul preached in Galatia, Jews there who rejected the gospel responded with malice. They pursued Paul from city to city, resulting in at least one physical attack that nearly killed him.*

Have someone read **Galatians 6:1–18** aloud, or have a few readers take turns. Then discuss the questions below:

Examine the approach to believers who have sinned in verses 1–5. What do you appreciate about the kind of character required to take that approach?

The false teachers invested in puffing up their own credentials. What makes the investments described in verses 6–10 different—and hard for you to do?

---

* See Acts 13:48—14:20.

Look at the boasting of the false teachers and of Paul in verses 11–18. How have you engaged in each kind of boasting?

This lesson's article will focus on the passage's emphasis on doing good, which Paul mentioned earlier as a part of the fruit of the Spirit. Take turns reading the article aloud, and then discuss the questions that follow.

ACTIONS AND CONSEQUENCES

5 MINUTES

Before moving to north Georgia, I lived in a farming community where planters would take seed and bury it in the ground, expecting a harvest of much more than was planted. It sounds like a risky business. But most often, those farms turn rows of dirt into rows of corn, cotton, and soybeans. There's a return on investment.

Paul uses this concept of investment with the Galatians. The principle involves letting go in order to gain. This works in many areas of life, from farming to stock investments to relationships—and in our spiritual lives. Every investment brings a return: a good investment brings a good return, and a poor investment brings a poor return. Or to put it in theological terms, righteousness and sin have consequences.

Are we investing in the care and feeding of our souls? What spiritual harvest are we expecting? We need to understand why we struggle to invest in our spiritual lives the way we do with our material lives. Why might we devote much to an exercise regimen or entertainment, but relatively little toward advancing the kingdom of Christ?

Imagine two fields that grow different crops. I get to choose which of these fields I will invest in with my God-given time, talents, and treasure. As I make these decisions, two voices compete for my loyalty: the flesh and the Holy Spirit. Which investment advisor will I follow?

The flesh makes grand promises concerning a worldly return on investment. It offers position, popularity, power, wealth, health, pleasure, and comfort. It makes me think these are the ways to joy and fulfillment. This worldly harvest may look amazing for a while, but eventually it rots and produces a dividend of destruction.

The harvest of the Spirit may not look as glorious right now, but the long-term return is a treasure stored up for eternal life. Actions have consequences. I reap what I sow. This is true in my personal spiritual life, in my marriage, with my children, in my workplace—everywhere I am called to invest.

Paul writes, "So then, as we have opportunity, let us do good to everyone, and especially to those who are of the household of faith" (v. 10). With this instruction to love each other like we are family, we need to be honest about how hard it is to love those closest to us. We are more aware of their sins than anyone else's. It requires extraordinary humility and mercy for family relationships to co-exist without exploding.

Healthy family and church dynamics depend on the *power* of the Spirit to bring love to bear as a *fruit* of the Spirit. The world is watching how we treat each other. Unbelievers are not judging us by the correctness of our theological positions but by whether we are kind or hostile, forgiving or resentful, vindictive or merciful. Jesus prayed for the Father to give us unity "so that the world may believe that you have sent me" (John 17:21). Divisiveness in the family of God undermines the church's ambassadorship for Jesus in the world.

We also are called to apply the doing-good principle to how we treat those who are not Christians. We do not view them as enemies, but as people we are called to serve, love, bless, and offer the living hope of God's transforming grace. This means doing good to undeserving and unworthy people who have no desire to do good to us. It goes against the grain of the flesh and is altogether counterintuitive to how the world operates.

But isn't this exactly how Jesus has treated you and me? By his mercy and kindness he blessed his enemies, turning us into brothers and sisters in the family of God. Our treason deserves the death penalty but, wonder of wonders, Jesus serves our sentence. He deserved honor and blessing and kindness, but received rebuke and rejection and condemnation, all so we would know the grace and love of the Father.

The cross teaches us that actions have consequences. Yes, *my* actions have consequences. But thankfully, so do the actions of Jesus! His sacrificial act overturned all of my sinful acts. It reconciled me to God as a fully forgiven, beloved child.

You see, the cross was God's investment strategy. He designed it to produce a harvest for himself from the blood of Christ. *You* are the return on investment the Father, Son, and Spirit most deeply desired. You no longer have to live as a spiritual orphan. Your own Abba, the Sovereign Lord, loves you so much he invested the very lifeblood of Jesus to reconcile you to himself as his own.

Wherever we look in Scripture and find doing-good principles, it will not take long to realize that you and I have not done the good required. But Jesus has! That grace becomes the motivation and power to invest in a new way. That's Paul's call to action: "As we have opportunity, let us do good." Ah, opportunity. For those who will rest in Jesus as their perfect righteousness, empowering grace will be available for every opportunity that presents itself.

All we need to do is open our eyes. Whether at home, for a friend or neighbor, or around the world, there are so many opportunities to do good to others—to make an investment for Christ's kingdom. How are you representing Jesus? How is your in-person presence (or your online one) a missional outpost? It begins with delighting in Jesus for yourself, as he delights in you.

DISCUSSION *10 MINUTES*

If someone examined your investments of time, talents, and treasure, what kind of return on investment would they think you seek?

What is a visible way you invest in Christ's kingdom, or how might you?

Lesson

EXERCISE

APPROACHING LIFE'S COMMON CONCERNS

20 MINUTES

The final chapter of Paul's letter to the Galatians gives an overall picture of the difference between a flesh-based life and a Spirit-based life—their opposite beliefs, attitudes, motives, and actions. It shows how each way of living approaches many of life's day-to-day concerns.

To close out your time studying Galatians, renew your hope in being Spirit-led by reading through the items below on your own. Each is drawn from Galatians 6 and addresses a commonplace issue in life. Note some where the Spirit is working in you or where you especially want to grow to become more Spirit-led. Although you will be honestly assessing your spiritual faults and need for growth, focus on the person you are becoming with the Spirit's help. Be ready to share some of your responses.

Approach to THE FAULTS OF OTHERS

The flesh. I heap burdens or shame on others for their faults, or I add pressure for them to become better, like the false teachers "who would force you" (v. 12).

The Spirit. My sense of my own need for the cross lets me confront and restore others "in a spirit of gentleness" (v. 1).

Approach to TEMPTATION

The flesh. I am seldom watchful. I figure I'm more resistant to sin than others, or sin is not really a danger I feel like taking seriously.

The Spirit. I remain humble and aware that I might fall into sin, staying close to Jesus: "Keep watch on yourself" (v. 1).

Approach to MY TIME AND MONEY

The flesh. I invest what I have in order to gain security, comforts, and approval for myself and/or my family.

The Spirit. I invest in Christ's kingdom, seeking its gain, even at a temporary cost to myself in this world.

Approach to BEING NOTICED

The flesh. I feel a need to "make a good showing" (v. 12), so that when people look at me they notice my devotion—a subtle way of boasting in myself.

The Spirit. I want people to notice Jesus. My only boast is how much I need the cross and what my Savior has done for me.

Approach to SUCCESS

The flesh. I play by the world's rules to be successful and avoid persecution. This means the world's threats, lures, and promises have power over me.

The Spirit. The Holy Spirit has power in me. The world's lures are dead to me—crucified!—as my focus is on being "a new creation" (v. 15) remade in Christ.

Approach to OTHER CULTURES

The flesh. I keep people who are different from me distant. I am uninterested, scornful, or fearful.

The Spirit. Christ's mission to come for me propels me to take the gospel even where I might feel out of place, and to "do good to everyone" (v. 10).

Approach to SUFFERING

The flesh. I am unwilling to risk mistreatment or suffering for Jesus, careful to make sure I will "not be persecuted for the cross of Christ" (v.12)

The Spirit. I am willing to undergo persecution, and I endure suffering as a person whose Savior suffered also: "I bear on my body the marks of Jesus" (v. 17).

Approach to CONTENTMENT

The flesh. I do not really know peace, as I am always hounded by something more I must do or some further safeguard I must construct.

The Spirit. I learn to rest in Christ who promises to all who trust him alone, "Peace and mercy be upon them" (v. 16).

When the group is ready, share some of your responses. How do you especially hope to grow into a more Spirit-led way of living? What are some specific ways your life might look different?

What gospel truth about Jesus and who you are in him will you especially have to see and believe so you can grow?

WRAP-UP AND PRAYER *10 MINUTES*

Pray together that God would keep growing you by his Word, using your study of Galatians to work his grace into your life. If your group is going to keep meeting now that this study is done, you might want to discuss plans for your next time together.

LEADER'S NOTES

These notes provide some thoughts and background information that connect to the discussion questions in each lesson's Bible conversation section. The discussion leader should read these notes before the study begins. Sometimes, the leader may want to refer the group to a point found here.

However, it is important that you not treat these notes as a way to look up the "right answer." The most helpful and memorable answers usually will be those the group discovers on its own through reading and thinking about the Bible text. You will lose the value of taking time to look thoughtfully at the text if you are too quick to turn to these notes.

LESSON 1: THE JESUS-PLUS EQUATION

Paul's letter is written against the backdrop of events described in Acts 13:13–16:5, where Paul preaches in Galatia and then is involved in the Judaizing controversy that leads to the council at Jerusalem. That entire account in Acts is probably too long for your whole group to read together. But as the leader, you might want to be familiar with those happenings so you are able to refer the group to particular details or briefly explain those events.

Paul's introduction of himself as an apostle (literally, a "sent one") is particularly strong in Galatians. He emphasizes that his authority and sending come straight from our death-defying God (see 1:11–12; Acts 9:1–16), as opposed to the humanly-generated views of the Judaizers. In this he has the support of the other leaders ("the brothers") of the church. Paul also describes himself as a preacher of the gospel (vv. 6–9) and a servant of Christ (v. 10). Despite holding much authority, he is not using that authority to advance his own interests but to promote Jesus and the gospel. This makes a powerful platform for godly leadership, from which he can write boldly.

This gospel-centeredness is not just a principle for Paul, but also his personal joy and navigational star. The foundation of everything he will write in Galatians is Jesus, risen from the dead, "who gave himself for our sins to deliver us from the present evil age" (v. 4). The Galatians would have known this message, since cross-and-resurrection was the centerpiece doctrine wherever Paul preached (see 1 Corinthians 2:2), including in Galatia (see Acts 13:26–41). Believers have been rescued from a pit of condemnation we could never escape on our own, and this fuels both Paul's mission and his personal praise.

This is also why adding human requirements to the gospel is so deplorable. It puts us back in the pit, trusting ourselves to find a way out, and unable to succeed. It also takes the praise and credit due Jesus and imagines some piece of it might apply to us: we can feel superior about our right theology, proper lifestyle, spiritual sentimentality, or ministry success. Paul will allow none of this. He rightly curses it, and points us to Christ alone.

LESSON 2: FACT-CHECKING THE GOSPEL

Paul's insistence that he didn't confer with the other apostles while learning the gospel may seem odd at first, but it fits his status as a prophet who speaks directly from God and is commissioned to write Scripture (see 2 Peter 3:15–16). Paul's own life was a miracle of grace, defined by a turnaround orchestrated solely by God. Having shown Paul amazing mercy in his life, the Lord then directly taught him the doctrines of that grace. Human ideas of salvation always include some form of self-reliance, so that the true gospel of an unearned rescue could only have been fashioned by God. The Lord reveals this gospel to Paul, and Paul displays an attitude about it that the Lord approves in Isaiah 66:2 when he commends "he who is humble and contrite in spirit and trembles at my word."

The Lord also gave Paul a specific missionary assignment. While the other apostles focused on preaching to Jews who already knew of the true God, Paul was to preach the gospel "to the uncircumcised," meaning the Gentiles (see Acts 22:21; 26:16–18). Despite their very different cultural contexts, though, Paul says the gospel he and the other apostles preached was identical. So too were the central applications of the gospel, such as a concern for the poor, who may have mostly been Jewish converts living in the Jerusalem area (see Paul's efforts in Romans 15:25–28 and 1 Corinthians 16:1–4). Jewish and Gentile believers receive the same gospel, have the same hope in Christ, and treat each other as members of the same heavenly family—sharing their money.

LESSON 3: GOSPEL COACHING

At the surface level, Peter (Cephas) was sinning by breaking off fellowship with the Gentile believers. But as is always the case, the heart of his sin ran deeper. Peter was idolizing the approval of the men from James, selfishly seeking it even though this meant being unkind to the Gentile believers and a bad influence on his fellow Jews. He was also giving in to fear, letting his concern for the opinions of influential people jeopardize the missionary work in Antioch and the purity of the gospel message for the Gentiles. But deeper still, Peter was being a gospel hypocrite. Although he knew that being right with God is not based on works of the law, he was not acting in line with this truth and may have struggled to embrace it emotionally. Functionally, he was not believing the gospel.

Paul saw this, and his approach was not merely to correct Peter's behavior but to call him back to unbending gospel faith. The glory of the gospel of grace will rectify Peter's error. Paul is not afraid to get theological, reflecting on the meaning of the cross, the basis for justification, and the relationship of these things to God's law. Notice that Paul confronts Peter in front of the other believers who were sinning along with him. Getting the gospel right, and acting in line with it, are important matters that deserve upfront attention.

For Paul, the believers in Antioch, or any of us, this gospel means our old selves are dead and supplanted by Jesus's life in us. Our burden to earn God's favor by our obedience is dead, and Christ's perfect obedience on our behalf lives. Our self-first priorities are dead, and Christ's priorities live. Our reliance on ourselves to achieve this godly life is dead, and Jesus's power in us lives. Our fear of human opinions is dead, and Jesus's courage to love lives.

Paul's argument in verses 17–19 may be hard to follow. He writes, "But if, in our endeavor to be justified in Christ, we too were found to be sinners, is Christ then a servant of sin? Certainly not! For if I rebuild what I tore down, I prove myself to be a transgressor. For through the law I died to the law, so that I might live to God." Paul's point is that being justified in Christ alone frees him to eat with Gentile believers. This can't possibly mean that eating with Gentiles is a sin, as the Judaizers claim, because it's a siding-with-Christ behavior and Christ is never in league with sin. The actual sin would be to rebuild the old Jewish requirements and add them to faith in Christ. In fact, the law itself condemned Paul in his old practice of trying to earn righteousness, and pointed him to Jesus instead. This frees him from that self-focused burden, letting him truly live for God.

LESSON 4: THE ANCIENT BLESSING

Paul labels the right approach to God as being "by the Spirit." Living by the Spirit means a relationship with God that's about receiving from him. God works salvation for us and gives it to us when we hear the gospel and believe, as the Spirit's creative and life-producing power works in us. The other approach to God is living "by works of the law," also called "by the flesh." In this approach, we imagine God demands to receive from us. We try to earn salvation or approval by our own obedience or superior status, and we try to grow as Christians by our own willpower. The flesh approach is so engrained in our remaining sinfulness that it's easy to slip into it even after we first receive the gospel with joy over how it's purely a gift. The Galatians had begun by receiving (v. 2) from "he who supplies" (v. 5), and even endured some suffering for the joy of that release, but still shifted back into an earning approach under the Judaizers' teaching.

The receiving approach has been our only hope ever since Adam's first sin, and has been good news all that time. It is good news that righteousness is by faith, not demanding our perfectly constant obedience. It is good news that faith itself comes from receiving the Spirit's life-giving work, not from conjuring up enough sincerity by our own strength. It is good news that God's gift of righteousness is a worldwide plan of blessing, not limited to one particular heritage. Even God's law serves the good news and may be heard with gladness. It teaches us the good works we are created in Christ to do, even as it reveals our failure before God and points us to Jesus the law keeper and curse bearer.

We can get so used to saying Jesus died for our sins that we miss the gravity of what this means: his place swapped with ours. It means he died to redeem us from sin's curse by becoming the curse we deserve, and it means he died to give us his righteousness by taking on the shame from our disobedience. We also might miss the full scope of the salvation Christ accomplishes, limiting it to personal forgiveness. But Paul says Christ died to bring all nations into the promises given to Abraham. Redemptive blessings the Bible specifically associates with Abraham include adoption as children of God (3:26–29), resurrection from the dead (Hebrews 11:17–19), and the inheritance of a heavenly life with God (Hebrews 11:8–16). Paul also says Christ died to give believers the promised Spirit. This means a life of knowing God's presence and one marked by his transforming power, beginning in this world and perfected in the next.

LESSON 5: GOD'S MIRROR

Paul gives many ways God's promises made to Abraham are unrivaled: they predate the law, cannot be annulled, and were made directly by God. More fundamentally, they are redemptive promises. They are part of God's eternal plan to save his people throughout the world by granting righteousness through faith, freeing them from the guilt and power of sin. The crowning wonder of these promises is that ultimately they are made to Jesus himself. The fact that we who have faith in him also share in the promises because we are Christ's (v. 29) reveals how fully we are joined to him. Our inheritance, our future glory, and our eternal life with God cannot be in doubt because Jesus surely has these treasures—and we have him.

Paul uses the imagery of imprisonment when he writes about God's law. The law found in Scripture leaves us trapped in sin if we think obeying it is the path to salvation. That performance-based way of relating to God can feel like a jail cell (and it *is* one if we don't turn to Christ in faith). In fact, Paul pointed out earlier in verse 10 that the law itself condemns us even as it tells us how to obey God. Thankfully, the law also anticipates our failure and points us to the coming Savior. Since the law's insufficiency to save is the main point of the passage, this probably is what Paul means when he says the law "was added because of transgressions" (v. 19). Although the law surely is useful in restraining sin and teaching us what a godly life looks like, its first use is to reveal our sin so that we turn to the Savior. Because of our sin, we need the law to convict us.

This way of relating to God that's based on promise rather than on law actually leads to a more rigorous obedience—and a redemptive one.

Trying to earn salvation through obedience leads only to an estranged relationship with God. But receiving his promises by faith leads to a reconciled relationship with God. Out of the joy, confidence, and power of that ongoing relationship we are freed to obey our Father in the wholehearted, loving way he commanded for our good all along.

LESSON 6: WEARING CHRIST

Paul's earlier imagery of the law bringing imprisonment now gives way to the similar image of slavery. It is not that the Old Testament laws are inherently bad commands. In Romans 7:12, Paul affirms that "the law is holy, and the commandment is holy and righteous and good." But the very goodness of those commands condemns us all in our sin if we are trusting our obedience to justify us. This performance mindset is the basic principle of the world, an approach all people are born into whether or not they know the commands of the Bible. It brings anxiety, blame, a resistance to faith, and a selfish compulsion to prove oneself right and get ahead at the expense of others—in a phrase, spiritual slavery. Only our sonship in Christ brings freedom from this, since only a child of the one perfect Father is secure in perfect love, protection, provision, access to God, discipline that is unwaveringly kind, and a heavenly home. A slave worries every day that the master's favor might be revoked if he should fail, and so the slave serves out of self-interest and grudging duty. A child of God has a secure inheritance and knows the Father's guidance is warmhearted, and is delighted to serve out of love.

LESSON 7: LIFE ON THE GOSPEL HIGHWAY

Although believers do put effort into the Christian life, faith in Jesus is not about trying but rather about relying. The Galatians were relying on their law keeping rather than relying on Christ's work for them. This made even their best effort fundamentally "weak and worthless" (v. 9). It was no better than their old pagan practices, since slavery to performance was its basis. Paul says that if they don't turn away from this misplaced reliance, his entire missionary effort with them will have been in vain. Legalism is *that* false and condemnable.

The impulse to earn favor by performing for God also leads to selfish behavior. Even if we outwardly seem to be caring much for others, we have an agenda focused on building ourselves up with whatever affirmation we feel we need secure. In contrast, the early relationship between Paul and the Galatians was marked by true concern and sacrifice. They would have given anything for him, and he is in loving anguish over the prospect of their falling away.

A core feature of the gospel is that is comes solely by God's promise to those who understand they can do nothing to bring salvation to themselves. Jesus is for the lowly. He rescues those who have given up on the world's ways and those whom the world has given up on: "He has brought down the mighty from their thrones and exalted those of humble estate" (Luke 1:52). Hagar and Sarah make a good example of the difference between self-effort and faith, even though Hagar may show some evidence of faith in the Genesis account and God shows repeated kindness toward her (see Genesis 16:7–14; 21:15–21). Paul's comment that Hagar and Sarah "may be interpreted allegorically" (Galatians 4:24) does not mean we may strip Scripture of its nature as an actual historical account, nor that we may read into it whatever moral lessons or symbolic references we care to imagine. God did arrange events to have symbolic meanings at times, but Paul's use of Hagar and Sarah to illustrate self-reliance versus God-reliance fits the spiritual message of Genesis as that part of the Bible records the events of their lives. Paul is not reading his own ideas into Genesis, but is being taught by Genesis.

NOTE ON THE WORD *SLAVE*: The labels Paul uses for himself (in 1:10) and for some Galatian believers (in 3:28), which are often translated as "slave," need a little explanation. Throughout Galatians,

Paul uses a group of words (mostly *doulos*, but also *paidiske* with reference to Hagar) that can be translated variously as "servant," "slave," or "bondservant." The terms all indicate a person who is subject to do work assigned by a master. This was a life-defining status within ancient Greco-Roman culture. Often, over time, a *doulos* could earn enough to purchase freedom. In some cases, a *doulos* would even choose to remain part of a master's household. It is important to recognize that this institution, which was still prone to sin and abuse, was very different from the race-based, chattel slavery that was practiced in Europe and the Americas later in history.

LESSON 8: THE KNOT OF GRACE

The freedom that Paul preaches is freedom from the crushing obligation to please God through law-keeping and religious observances, which only ends slavery to our failure. It does not mean Jesus has freed us from any moral obligations at all, as if God is fine with us doing whatever feels good at the moment whether godly or not. Being out from under the law actually frees us to live in a truly selfless manner, no longer anxious about our own performance. Paul still advocates a godly life when he mentions love in verses 6 and 13, and he affirms one of the Bible's main summaries of God's moral law when he writes, "You shall love your neighbor as yourself" (v. 14).

The danger of those who pushed circumcision was that they destroyed this freedom. An indifferent matter like circumcision, or even a good practice, becomes an enemy of Christ when it is a way we try to earn salvation by completing certain obligations. It becomes a return to the slavery of our own performance, which is a rejection of Christ's performance on our behalf. When God instituted circumcision, he drew on the cutting-off imagery inherent in the rite by declaring, "Any uncircumcised male who is not circumcised in the flesh of his foreskin shall be cut off from his people; he has broken my covenant" (Genesis 17:14). Here in Galatians, Paul says the legalistic misuse of circumcision cuts a person off from Christ (v. 4). It is a rejection of his grace, and a denial of the hope we have in his righteousness alone.

This gospel insistence that our own efforts contribute nothing to salvation is offensive to those who wish to save themselves. But any teaching that imagines a superior class of believers based on pride in religious observances is offensive to the cross, where all sins are equally forgiven and Jesus's righteousness is equally given. Paul leaves no doubt what he thinks of that.

LESSON 9: THE FLESH-KILLING SPIRIT

Participants may want to see where Paul uses *sarx* ("the flesh") to mean both religious self-reliance and rebellious self-gratification. The religious expression of the flesh is first found in 3:3, "Having begun by the Spirit, are you now being perfected by the flesh?" The rebellious expression of the flesh is found here in chapter 5. The point of seeing that they are the same word (which also can simply mean a human body, as in 2:20) is to realize that they are not really so different. Both religious self-effort and outright immorality are sinful human impulses that resist Christ. Our tendency sometimes is to try to correct religious legalism by allowing some moral laxness, but this just trades one expression of the flesh for another. Likewise, we cannot free ourselves from the flesh by trying to battle corrupt behavior with religious self-effort.[6]

The freedom Paul has written so much about is a freedom *from* the flesh and a freedom *to* serve others. The idea of service might sound like a strange view of freedom, but it makes sense when we remember that sin kept us in bondage to self-interest. We are now freed to be like Jesus, who said, "I am among you as the one who serves" (Luke 22:27). What glory is ours! With the freedom to love our neighbor as ourselves, the law that reveals God's beauty is lived out in us.

This is one reason the works of the flesh include both sins against God directly (idolatry, sorcery) and sins against our neighbor (anger, rivalries). A love for God naturally includes a love for neighbor because love is a Godlike quality, while rejection of God leaves us without his power to be like him. Also, both idolatry and dissension among each other result from the urge to fashion and safeguard our own credentials before God, which was the paramount problem in the Galatians churches. With some believers trying to hold onto the idea that they had made themselves better than others, it is not surprising that there was strife and jealousy, and this may be why Paul mentions several sins that surround conflict. When we follow our own made-up ideas for how to be blessed, even clear sensual evils (drunkenness, orgies) fit our underlying attitude toward God. We're doing what feels good to us rather than receiving God's blessings in his way.

The fruit of the Spirit makes a delightful contrast. Each of the qualities mentioned is repeatedly associated with the character of God all through the Bible. Everyone who walks by the Spirit receives an invaluable gift: the freedom to reflect God's own excellence and glory.

LESSON 10: DOING GOOD AND BEARING SCARS

The gentleness toward those caught in sin is the same quality Jesus spoke of to describe his heart toward sinners: "I am gentle and lowly in heart, and you will find rest for your souls" (Matthew 11:29). We should treat a sinner like Jesus would treat that sinner. And if Jesus who never sinned took a lowly posture, we who are sinners ourselves should take a humble approach to other sinners. Before being quick to scold them for their condition, we ought to check our own. Are we filled with sympathy like Jesus? Is our motive to administer grace, or have we come to gloat? Paul specifies that correction should be done by "you who are spiritual" (v. 1), meaning those who know the grace and power of the cross in their own lives. Spiritual believers are also watchful, aware of how easily sin deceives anyone including themselves. They do not approach ensnared people with a sense of superiority.

When Paul says a believer should test his own work so that "his reason to boast will be in himself alone and not his neighbor" (v. 4), he does not mean we should boast as if we have earned religious superiority. Rather, he is condemning the false teachers who were so sure they were already righteous that they turned their attention to shortcomings they saw in others, taking additional pride in getting others to be like them. We should instead be humbly focused only on how God is working even in someone like us. Then our real boast will be in Christ.

When he is all our life and reputation, we have a stake in his kingdom. We will invest in hearing God's Word. And we will be tireless about doing good to others, both nearby and far away, which shows that God's kingdom is breaking into our present world. Although it is glorious to be part of this, the glory is often veiled. Christ's kingdom is a kingdom of humble service. It does not conform to the world's expectations about power and prestige.

Any supposedly Christian endeavor that fails to recognize this, and instead boasts in things that "make a good showing in the flesh" (v. 12), is not of God. The false teachers took pride in their circumcision, which made them appear devoted to God. But Paul's body shows marks of suffering and humility: "I bear on my body the marks of Jesus" (v. 17). In people trying to earn religious approval, scars from persecution might be shown off as evidence of their superior devotion, but Paul doesn't speak of his scars that way. Instead, he constantly speaks of Christ's life and the Spirit's power in him. Paul's marks of Jesus are evidence that God has claimed him. In God's power and grace, even a former persecutor like Paul can become one who is willing to be persecuted—for Christ, and like Christ.

NOTES

1. Jack Miller's way of summarizing the gospel by noting how sin is worse than we think but grace is better than we think lives on in Serge resources such as *Sonship* (Greensboro, NC: New Growth Press, 2013), 1–4.

2. Elements of this exercise are adapted from the "Law and the Gospel" lesson in Serge's *Sonship* (Greensboro, NC: New Growth Press, 2013), 60–61.

3. The description of the civil law as being expired is the wording used by *The Westminster Confession of Faith*, 19.4.

4. The use of the Lord's Prayer is adapted from an earlier resource in the Gospel-Centered Life series authored by Rose Marie Miller, Deborah Harrell, and Jack Klumpenhower, *The Gospel-Centered Parent* (Greensboro, NC: New Growth Press, 2015), 52–53.

5. Corey Kilgannon, "Sidewalk Is His Prison Yard," *New York Times*, March 11, 2011.

6. Some of the language used to explain the two expressions of the flesh is borrowed from Serge's Discipleship Lab materials. To learn more about this training, visit serge.org/discipleship-lab/.

mission

propelled by God's Grace

Go and grow with us.

Since 1983, Serge has been helping individuals and churches engage in global mission. From short-term trips to long-term missions – we want to see the power of God's grace transform your own life and motivate and sustain you to move into the lives of others – particularly those who do not yet know Jesus.

As a sending agency we:

- **Take a gospel-centered approach to life and ministry**
- **Provide proactive Missionary Care**
- **Practice incarnational ministry**
- **Believe God works in our weakness**

Visit us online at:
serge.org/missions

Grace at the Fray

Gospel Renewal
fuels mission

Serge is...

As an international missions agency, we realize we need the grace of the gospel in our own lives, even as we take the message of God's grace to others. Our work consists of helping people experience on-going *gospel renewal* and equipping them to move outward into *mission*.

We seek to foster this transformation in ministry leaders, churches, and all believers around the world.

Visit us online at:
serge.org

MISSIONS | MENTORING | RESOURCES

Grace at the Fray

resources
for continued **spiritual growth**

We never outgrow our need for the gospel.

No matter where you are on your Christian journey, Serge resources help you live out the gospel in every part of your life and encourage the same growth in others. Whether you are a church leader, actively engaged in ministry, or just seeking to go deeper in your relationship with God - we have resources that can help.

- **Books and Studies**
- **Discipleship and Training**
- **Grace-Centered Teaching Events**
- **Webinars**
- **Podcast**

Visit us online at:
serge.org/renewal

Grace at the Fray